The Year of the Poet XI

February 2024

The Poetry Posse

inner child press, ltd.

The Poetry Posse 2024

Gail Weston Shazor
Shareef Abdur Rasheed
Teresa E. Gallion
hülya n. yılmaz
Noreen Snyder
Tzemin Ition Tsai
Elizabeth Esguerra Castillo
Jackie Davis Allen
Mutawaf Shaheed
Caroline 'Ceri' Nazareno
Ashok K. Bhargava
Alicja Maria Kuberska
Swapna Behera
Albert 'Infinite' Carrasco
Michelle Joan Barulich
Eliza Segiet
William S. Peters, Sr.

~ * ~

In order to maintain each poet's authentic voice, this volume has not undergone the scrutiny of editing. Please take time to indulge each contributor for their own creativity and aspirations to convey their uniqueness.

hülya n. yılmaz, Ph.D.
Director of Editing ~
Inner Child Press International

General Information

The Year of the Poet X
February 2024 Edition

The Poetry Posse

1ˢᵗ Edition : 2024

This Publishing is protected under Copyright Law as a "Collection". All rights for all submissions are retained by the Individual Author and or Artist. No part of this Publishing may be Reproduced, Transferred in any manner without the prior **WRITTEN CONSENT** of the "Material Owners" or its Representative Inner Child Press. Any such violation infringes upon the Creative and Intellectual Property of the Owner pursuant to International and Federal Copyright Laws. Any queries pertaining to this "Collection" should be addressed to Publisher of Record.

Publisher Information
1ˢᵗ Edition : Inner Child Press
intouch@innerchildpress.com
www.innerchildpress.com

Copyright © 2024 : The Poetry Posse

ISBN-13 : 978-1-961498-16-7 (inner child press, ltd.)

$ 12.99

WHAT WOULD
LIFE
BE WITHOUT
A LITTLE
POETRY?

Dedication

This Book is dedicated to

Humanity, Peace & Poetry

the Power of the Pen

can effectuate change!

&

The Poetry Posse

past, present & future,

our Patrons and Readers &

the Spirit of our Everlasting Muse

In the darkness of my life
I heard the music
I danced . . .
and the Light appeared
and I dance

Janet P. Caldwell

Table of Contents

Foreword .... *ix*

Preface .... *xiii*

Renowned Poets .... *xv*

   Omar Khayyam

The Poetry Posse

Gail Weston Shazor	1
Alicja Maria Kuberska	7
Jackie Davis Allen	13
Tezmin Ition Tsai	19
Shareef Abdur – Rasheed	25
Noreen Snyder	31
Elizabeth Esguerra Castillo	37
Mutawaf Shaheed	43
hülya n. yılmaz	51
Teresa E. Gallion	57
Ashok K. Bhargava	63
Caroline Nazareno-Gabis	69

Table of Contents . . . *continued*

Swapna Behera	75
Albert Carassco	83
Michelle Joan Barulich	89
Eliza Segiet	95
William S. Peters, Sr.	101

February's Featured Poets — 109

Caroline Laurent Turunç	111
Julio Pavanetti	119
Lidia Chiarelli	129
Lina Buividavičiūtė	125

Inner Child Press News — 145

Other Anthological Works — 183

Foreword

Renowned Poets

Omar Khayyam

Omar Khayyam (1048 - 1123) was a Persian poet, famous for his Rubaiyat form of poetry built upon quatrains. He was also a well-known philosopher, mathematician, astronomer, mystic and a free-thinker, who wondered about the impermanence of life, and man's relationship to God. He lived in a time period when fanaticism, orthodoxy and military demagogues controlled and dictated people's daily life. Through his poems, Khayyam encouraged people to break free from the socio-political and religious tyranny. Unfortunately, his poems could not be circulated openly due to a callous an intolerant environment. As a result, only few of his contemporaries had the chance to read and benefit from it.

He doubted the existence of divine providence and the afterlife and chose to put his faith in a joyful appreciation of the fleeting and sensuous beauties of the material world to celebrate the idyllic nature and pleasures of living in a moment as below:

Set not thy heart on any good or gain,
life means but pleasure,
or means but pain;

when Time lets slip a little perfect hour,
O take it - for it will not come again.

Khayyam warned that if self-care is neglected and postponed to some obscure notion of 'tomorrow', the pleasure of living in the 'now' is irreversibly lost. He believed that each moment of life is complete in itself, by itself, and that the incompleteness manifests itself only in the 'mental state' of which we are not often aware. The natural world lives independently for itself, unattached to our feelings of pain and joy, and in Khayyam's view, acknowledging this liberating fact is the first step towards having a pleasant life. He said not to take things too seriously and to question existence of God and heaven:

Grab life with both your hands,
squeeze every bit it has to offer,
cherish it every day.
For what else is there?

Some scholars and critics argue that the name of Omar Khayyam should "be struck out from the history of Persian literature" due to the lack of any material that could confidently be attributed to him. While it is certain that Khayyam wrote many quatrains, it is hardly possible, save in a few exceptional cases, to assert positively that he wrote any of those ascribed to him.

The modern-day popularity of Khayyam is mainly due to the English translations of Edward FitzGerald (1859) from the Bodleian manuscript.

Ashok K. Bhargava

President, Writers International Network Canada
Vancouver, BC

Coming April 2024

www.innerchildpress.com/world-healing-world-peace-poetry

Preface

We, **Inner Child Press International, The Year of the Poet** and **The Poetry Posse** welcome you.

WOW . . . a decade. We are so excited as we have now crossed over into our 11th year of *The Year of the Poet*.

This particular year we have chosen to feature renowned poets of history. We do hope you enjoy. Read ~ Learn.

For those of you who are not familiar with our story, back in 2013, a few of us poets got together with the simple intention of producing a book a month. That was our challenge. Since that time the enterprise has blossomed and brought forth a fruit that seems to keep on growing as evidenced as we enter 2023.

Our purpose is simple. Through our lyrical words and verse, we not only wish to share our poetic works, but we also have the poetic naiveté to believe that we can assist in the growth of consciousness of the things that have an effect our collective humanity. Therefore, we welcome your readership. For more about what we are attempting to accomplish, have a look at our Publishing Web Site . . . www.innerchildpress.com. If you would like to know a bit more about this particular endeavor please stop by for a visit at :

www.innerchildpress.com/the-year-of-the-poet

Over the years, Inner Child Press has been socially active to bring awareness and catalog through literature the things that have an impact upon our world and its inhabitants. We have solicited, produced, underwritten and published quite a few volumes to that end. For more insight you may wish to visit : www.innerchildpress.com/the-anthology-market. If you are a writer, poet, or activist, you would be advised to keep a eye out for upcoming volumes should you desire to participate. All readers are welcomed as well. Note, that there is a myriad of published volumes that are available as a FREE PDF download as well as available for purchase at affordable prices.

We at this time extend to you our well wishes for your own personal journey and hope that you consider including us as a travel companion.

Bless Up

Bill

William S. Peters, Sr.

Publisher
Inner Child Press International
www.innerchildpress.com

Renowned Poets
Omar Khayyam
1753 ~ 1784

February 2024

by hülya n. yılmaz, Ph.D.

Oh, come with old Khayyam, and leave the Wise
To talk; one thing is certain, that Life flies;
One thing is certain, and the Rest is Lies;
The Flower that once has blown forever dies.

From the Rubaiyat of Omar Khayyam (1048-1123), as translated with an adaptation in 1859 by Edward Fitzgerald (1809-1883)

In this February, 2024 issue of *The Year of the Poet*, we focus on the Persian Omar Khayyam, a polymath, known for his contributions to mathematics, astronomy, philosophy, and poetry. During his lifetime, which he spent under the rule of the Seljuk Empire, he attained fame foremost as an astronomer and a mathematician. Only after his death, his poetry became widely known. His *Rubaiyat*, titled thus in translation, may be said to be his most famous work of poetry, a collection of 1,200 to 2,000 quatrains.

This Islamic scholar influenced the world with his work in geometric algebra, the Jalil calendar—a calendar reform, his philosophy—in line with traditional Islamic eschatological doctrine, his compilation of astronomical tables, and his poetry.

In the West, his poems were assumed to play on sensual delights. In stark contrast to this outsider view, a totally different understanding ruled over his poetry in the Islamic East; namely, as a sophisticated allegory of the soul's love for the Muslim God. The imagery Khayyam used in his poetic work was seen as mystical love, the love that consumed the Muslim mystic, Sufi, on his path to the Divine. Islamic mysticism, Sufism, is heavily soaked in his *Rubaiyat*. Wine, Saki—the wine bearer, and intoxication are repeated images Khayyam used in that voluminous collection of quatrains. The following excerpts translated by Edward Fitzgerald succinctly demonstrate his Sufi imagery, as comprehended accurately in the Islamic East:

[. . .]

Ah, my Beloved, fill the Cup that clears
Today of past Regrets and future Fears;
Tomorrow!—Why, Tomorrow I may be
Myself with Yesterday's Sev'n thousand Years.

[. . .]

Ah, make the most of what we may yet spend,
Before we too into the Dust descend;
Dust into Dust, and under Dust to lie,
Sans Wine, sans Song, sans Singer, and sans End!

The wine bearer ("my Beloved") Khayyam wrote about in the first quatrain quote represents the Islamic Divine, Allah. As for "the Cup", it is merely a bridge through which the Lover of the Divine attains Divine Love.

The second quatrain cited above might appear to Westerners to be about a worldy intoxication through sensual delights. It is, however, yet once again, an imagery through which Omar Khayyam situates himself into the path to Divine Love.

In the hope that we all understand that which is beyond the surface and whom that is under the cloak in actuality . . .

hülya n. yılmaz, Ph.D.

Professor Emerita, Penn State, U.S.A.
Director of Editing Services at
Inner Child Press International, U.S.A.

Poets . . .
sowing seeds in the
Conscious Garden of Life,
that those who have yet to come
may enjoy the Flowers.

Poets, Writers . . . know that we are the enchanting magicians that nourishes the seeds of dreams and thoughts . . . it is our words that entice the hearts and minds of others to believe there is something grand about the possibilities that life has to offer and our words tease it forth into action . . . for you are the Poet, the Writer to whom the Gift of Words has been entrusted . . .

~ wsp

Poetry succeeds where instruction fails.

~ wsp

Now Available

www.innerchildpress.com/the-anthology-market.com

Gail Weston Shazor

Gail Weston Shazor

Gail Weston Shazor is a lover of words. She is fond of the arcane, unusual and the not yet words.

Coining words at an early age, there was often a bit of trouble with teachers, but she always had her mother and aunt to back up her choices in expression. Born in Mississippi, she spent her early years with her grandparents. Each of the four left very careful influences on her pre-schooling. She learned in turn how women worked in and out of the home and how men worked in and out of the home to support the family. She learned that a lack of proper schooling was not the only way to learn and understanding life was a great teacher. As in most rural families of color, women had a greater chance of formal learning. Both of Gail's grandmothers read out loud to the family whether it was the bible or the newspapers and important documents to their spouses.

Gail Weston Shazor has authored (so far) Notes from the Blue Roof, A Overstanding of an Imperfect Love, HeartSongs and Lies My Grandfather's Told Me. The number of anthologies is too many to list with the premier accomplishment of one of the contributors to The Year of The Poet. Gail will always lend her ink to community projects and will purchase the books of fellow poets in the Inner Child Press family.

Sacredness Nonet

The

Spiral

Wounds its way

Into the core

Of our aching heart

And by no number known

We are seen in completion

Levels and stairs that each must trod

The soul must seek its own perfection

Stop

And just like that
The words ceased
The words unspoken and unwritten
The movements of syllables
Along the spines of books, unprinted
The everyday busy crowding
Writing
I miss you
I miss the languishing of participles
And the dangling off the edges
Of my memory
Where did the stories go
I have cleaned my space
Made room for letters
Dug out my notes
And I await your voice
While holding a pencil in my hand
Eyes narrowed in search
Of the quiet
Tears coursing my cheeks
Because I love you
Bless my mind
Please

Gail Weston Shazor

Comma…Synchronicity

I am a comma in my bed,
without a reason or purpose,
I lay.

Having once lost separation,
Between where your skin would meet mine,
In bed.

Curved together in peaceful rest,
Or jointedly in lustful dance,
As one.

The melody reverberates,
On the rib of Adam that made
His Eve.

The list of whys grow way too long.
My pause is better suited for,
Reason

For a painful separation;
Words relatively linked as one:
In love

~~~~~~~~~~~~~*~~~~~~~~~~~~~

Our language could have been rested,
And modified with new meaning:
Today

Without the harsh finality,
Of your use of a period,
I sleep.

Alicja Maria Kuberska

Alicja Maria Kuberska

Alicja Maria Kuberska – awarded Polish poetess, novelist, journalist, editor.

She is a member of the Polish Writers Associations in Warsaw, Poland and IWA Bogdani, Albania. She is also a member of directors' board of Soflay Literature Foundation, Our Poetry Archive (India) and Cultural Ambassador for Poland (Inner Child Press, USA)

Her poems have been published in numerous anthologies and magazines in : Poland, Czech Republic, Slovakia, Hungary,Ukraina, Belgium, Bulgaria, Albania, Spain, the UK, Italy, the USA, Canada, the UK, Argentina, Chile, Peru, Israel, Turkey, India, Uzbekistan, South Korea, Taiwan, China, Australia, South Africa, Zambia, Nigeria

She received two medals - the Nosside UNESCO Competition in Italy (2015) and European Academy of Science Arts and Letters in France (2017). Ahe also received a reward of international literary competition in Italy „ Tra le parole e 'elfinito" (2018). She was announced a poet of the 2017 year by Soflay Literature Foundation (2018).She also received : Bolesław Prus Prize Poland (2019), Culture Animator Poland (2019) and first prize Premio Internazionale di Poesia Poseidonia- Paestrum Italy (2019).

Omar Khayaam

Nishapur, May 31, 1048
- the first day of life
of a doctor, mathematician, astronomer,
philosopher and poet.
It did not end in December 1131.

Memory lasts and permeates eternity.
Someone wrote his name on a moon crater
and on an asteroid in the main asteroid belt.
It appears on the spines of the volumes
in many libraries and bookstores.

Wisdom does not pass away and says
that life still goes on in between
more cups of wine.

Rubaiyats whisper:
It's not worth worrying about the past,
look forward to days that may not come
and today has a sweet-tart taste.

They teach that youth will fade and love will shrivel
- they will be like a dried rose with sharp thorns.
Time will take everything and turn it into dust.

Before the last petal falls to the ground
you can see a piece of paradise on earth

Author's Evening

An old actress recites poems with emotion
and sings old hits in a broken voice.
Spectators, participants of the show,
reward every number with loud applause.

Time turned the girl
into a hunched woman.
It wrote down her memories
in a thick biography.
There is little left
of the artist's former beauty
- a few photos preserved her youth.

Past events come back in stories,
forgotten songs are resurrected,
the memory of former lovers revives
anecdotes whisper shameful secrets.

The old woman dances slowly on the stage.
She performs in a provincial theatre
- desperately looking
for echoes of applause and money.
The dead star has flashed sadly
for the last time.

Woman In A Red Dress

She went out onto the balcony
stood for a moment
and lit a cigarette

The breeze ruffled her hair
and a thin stream of blue smoke.
The dress was fluttering
 like a banner carried to the barricades

She hugged the wind
and they flew to meet the ground
- a purple flower
bloomed on the sidewalk

Someone screamed in terror,
the sound of an ambulance
cut through the silence.
She was lying on a concrete shield

She had won battles
but she lost the war.
Life didn't stop.
It went on.

Jackie Davis Allen

Jackie Davis Allen

Jackie Davis Allen, otherwise known as Jacqueline D. Allen or Jackie Allen, grew up in the Cumberland Mountains of Appalachia. As the next eldest daughter of a coal miner father and a stay at home mother, she was the first in her family to attend and graduate from college. Her siblings, in their own right, are accomplished, though she is the only one, to date, that has discovered the gift of writing.

Graduating from Radford University, with a Bachelor's of Science degree in Early Education, she taught in both public and private schools. For over a decade she taught private art classes to children both in her home and at a local Art and Framing Shop where she also sold her original soft sculptured Victorian dolls and original christening gowns.

She resides in northern Virginia with her husband, taking much needed get-aways to their mountain home near the Blue Ridge Mountains, a place that evokes memories of days spent growing up in the Appalachian Mountains.

A lover of hats, she has worn many. Following marriage to her college sweetheart, and as wife, mother, grandmother, teacher, tutor, artist, writer, poet and crafter, she is a lover of art and antiques, surrounding herself, always, with books, seeking to learn more.

In 2015 she authored *Looking for Rainbows, Poetry, Prose and Art*, and in 2017, *Dark Side of the Moon*. Both books of mostly narrative poetry were published by Inner Child Press and were edited by hulya n. yilmaz in 2019, *No Illusions. Through the Looking Glass*, which was nominated to be considered for a Pulitzer Prize by the publisher and editor of Inner Child Press, ltd.

http://www.innerchildpress.com/jackie-davis-allen.php
jackiedavisallen.com

Introspection

Dreaming of the heavens,
The stars astronomically
A million miles away,

My favorite pen,
Attempting to dip
Into the deep, incalculable dark-inks.

Inspired from reading
The epic poetry
of Omar Khayyam,

I realize I've far to go.
Theorizing, I am,
That such genius as his comes

Around infrequently. Actually, rarely,
As best as I can,
I'll seek to find my own way.

And from my heart-speaks,
My voice will sing:
May the spark that ignites passion,
Fuel and elevate my wings.

A Night Filled with Choices

Brilliant city lights, splendiferous.
Impassioned nights, precipitous,
Filled with alluring excitement.
Anticipating, considering possibilities.

Seductive, she pondered her response
To the young man with flashing eyes.
The one with the mysterious smile.
And decided upon a plan

Like bees attracted to pollen.
Indulgently, like bees to honey
Innocently, she desired
To offer her charms, exchanging them

For the chance to dance
To the music and to the beat.
She smiled at him.
And he began to shuffle his feet.

Attracted by his mysterious smile,
And by his shuffling feet,
She caught his eye.
He caught hers.

And the music faded into the night

Discovery

Inside

The club I went,

To search for my lover.

I motioned, he smiled.

They embraced.

I wept.

Tzemin
Ition
Tsai

Tzemin Ition Tsai

Dr. Tzemin Ition Tsai comes from the Republic of China(Taiwan). In addition to being a professor of literature at a university, he is more committed to writing poems, novels, and proses. He is also an editor of "Reading, Writing and Teaching" academic text, an International editor of "Contemporary dialogues" literary periodical in Macedonia, and Vice-Chairman of the International Jury of the SAHITTO INTERNATIONAL AWARD in Bangladesh, and a columnist for "Chinese Language Monthly" in Taiwan.

In a wide range of literary creations, he is particularly fond of interesting stories or novels, and writing articles or poems about the feelings of nature and human beings. He has won many national literary awards. His literary works have been anthologized and published in books, journals, and newspapers in more than 55 countries and have been translated into more than 24 languages.

Wilted Flower

In the forest, where once flowers were in bloom
A flower that stands alone
The petals are withered. The beauty is gone.
The wind whispers and sighs at her
Your beauty will be in my mind's eye,
But your soul will fly away to a place far, far away

The flower nods, even though it is now content
It still closes its eyes. It quietly accepts its fate.
Even though its petals once bloomed
It is lying, all alone, on the frosty ground of the forest.
Petals flying in all directions, petals flying in all directions one by one

Like being abandoned, that feeling of sadness and loneliness
The flower knows that this is not the end of it.
After a gap of year, this spring has bloomed again.
So the flower lie down and wait
The arrival of spring, when the morning sun rises again
To become beautiful once again

The Songstress In The Tavern

Lights in an inn have been dimmed,
A songstress is singing her heart out.
Her sound is like a bird in flight,
Don't wait for a night to give up.
The words in the song are like a poem,
Filled with beauty and sophistication,
Rather tell of loving and losing,
I don't want to hold on to the burning pain in my heart.

Now you are far away,
Wandering around on my own makes me feel frustrated.
The memories come back to give me some comfort,
But I am longing to keep my sanity.
The heart that you once touched and ached, I have no nourishment.
It has been a part of my life for a very long time.
I'll keep it sealed with beeswax,
Until I know that someday we will be together again.

A Landscape Of Fine Sand

With whispers kissed by the tide and choirs of seagulls,
My village nestles, a heart on the shore of the ocean.
Salt stained cobblestones paving ancient stories,
Where moonbeams dance and sun-kissed nets adore the sun.

Like brushstrokes on the blue, sun-bleached sails,
Unfurl dreams on the whispering wind's command.
The strong backs of father and comrades,
Etched maps of life and Earth.

Smell of salt air, fish drying on lines,
Echoes of laughter mingled with the tide.
Soft touches of the times on these weathered walls,
Whispering of generations gone by.

All village children,
Echoing the whispers of the future that will last forever.
The dream belonging to the village,
Like a symphony through the ages.

The waves sing hymns to the depths,
My heart eternally bound.
This jewel holds ancient secrets,
My little village forever and ever.

Shareef Abdur Rasheed

Shareef Abdur Rasheed

Shareef Abdur-Rasheed, AKA Zakir Flo was born and raised in Brooklyn, New York. His education includes Brooklyn College, Suffolk County Community College and Makkah, Saudi Arabia. He is a Veteran of the Viet Nam era, where in 1969 he reverted to his now reverently embraced Islamic Faith. He is very active in the Islamic community and beyond with his teachings, activism and his humanity.

Shareef's spiritual expression comes through the persona of "Zakir Flo" . Zakir is Arabic for "To remind". Never silent, Shareef Abdur-Rasheed is always dropping science, love, consciousness and signs of the time in rhyme.

Shareef is the Patriarch of the Abdur-Rasheed Family with 9 Children (6 Sons and 3 Daughters) and 41 Grandchildren (24 Boys and 17 Girls).

For more information about Shareef, visit his personal FaceBook Page at :

https://www.facebook.com/shareef.abdurrasheed1
https://zakirflo.wordpress.com

Khayyam

genius
master of numerous
sciences
aside from mathematics
astronomy, philosophy,
he was a prolific and
until today world renowned
poet
Came: 05/18/1048 Went:
12/04/1131
in Persia
known for his design of a
solar calendar known as
the Jalail calendar that
became the basis for the
Persian calendar to this day
his collection known as
' Quatrains' though somewhat
suspect as poetry instead
scholars regarded it as
quotations even so his stature
demanded respect therefore
his work is considered poetry
Omar Khayyam genius

Birdland..,

NYC, Broadway near fifty deuce 1949
American original gem introduced
a sound to listen to produced
and bebop let loose
into town Birdland flew
with that jazz sound new
for fifteen years jazz on the menu
flavor made the venue
where the best appeared there
the giants of yesterday year, mostly gone
but their contributions still here, live on
named after the " yardbird " himself
bird was there on the scene as was miles,
here, live, count,
here, live walked in to
and these are just a few that blew at that venue
where patrons of all social, economic strips hue
where right there in full view
mingled together with the Broadway, Hollywood types
but the likes of Broadway, Hollywood Louis,
the sugar man named Robinson weren't the hype
it was that sound that ambience
flavor unique one would think
this should be bottled to drink
my man Pee Wee the eminent MC barker
ladies and gents welcome to the jazz corner
of the world in the name of Charlie " Yardbird " Parker.
groovin all night with ' Stella by starlight ' way beyond
' round bout midnight ' we only have eyes for you

deeep..,

in the bowels earth's caverns heaved
something hard to believe
scum covered blood lovers
some believe never had mothers
bottom feeders rose up to be leaders
others eventually got to be in ships
crossing seas
raided motherland stole human beings
human beings died who
tried to escape
brought to work land devils take
treaties fake made to break
earth soaked in blood of the people
evil men steal use kidnapped souls to
pick earth's yield those stole souls bound
in steal
some believe these were ' good ol days ' for
real
buying ' n ' selling human beings let's make a deal
so, dam Amerikkka how would you feel
if the script flipped 4 real
and ya'll got to know how the whip feels?
on your back in the killing fields
maybe you become strange fruit
when the pendulum swings back to you

Noreen Snyder

Noreen Snyder

Noreen Ann Snyder has been writing since she was a teenager. She writes a variety of different topics. Her favorite poetic forms are Sonnets, Blitz, Haiku, Tanka, and Free Verse. She always learning different poetic forms.

Noreen Ann Snyder is a poet, writer, and an author of five books, (four books are co-authored with her late husband, Garry A. Snyder.) Her poetry is in several Inner Child Press Anthologies. She is the founder of The Poetry Club on Facebook.

Omar Khayyam

Omar was intelligent and wise man.
He wrote the Rubaiyat (Quatrains)
and famous quotes such as
"Be happy for this moment."
Omar was also a mathematician and astronomer.
He was known for his works in
geometric algebra and Jalil Calendar.
We can learn so much from him, a
a well-rounded man.

Sonnet 29

Four years ago today, you have left this
earth for Heaven, a better place to be
pain-free, wheelchair free, and you are in bliss
and I will always be your devotee.
I have learned to live without you but I
don't want to. Don't get me wrong, I'll always
love you and I will never say good-bye
and I do not want to. Let me rephrase.
If I had another day, if I could,
so much I want to do and want to say
while you were alive and you understand.
I wish I could love you, play, and pray.
This sonnet is for you and I will not
stop writing you, you're always in my thought.

We Wait

We wait patiently

until the storm blows over

the silence returns.

Elizabeth E. Castillo

Elizabeth Esguerra Castillo

Elizabeth Esguerra Castillo is a multi-awarded and an Internationally-Published Contemporary Author/Poet and a Professional Writer / Creative Writer / Feature Writer / Journalist / Travel Writer from the Philippines. She has 2 published books, "Seasons of Emotions" (UK) and "Inner Reflections of the Muse", (USA). Elizabeth is also a co-author to more than 60 international anthologies in the USA, Canada, UK, Romania, India. She is a Contributing Editor of Inner Child Magazine, USA and an Advisory Board Member of Reflection Magazine, an international literary magazine. She is a member of the American Authors Association (AAA) and PEN International.

Web links:

Facebook Fan Page

https://free.facebook.com/ElizabethEsguerraCastillo

Google Plus

https://plus.google.com/u/0/+ElizabethCastillo

The Rubaiyat

He awakens to a brand-new day

Constellations above are at bay,

The Rubaiyat dares to take flight

Ceases to be a mere phantom of the night.

His works changed the course of the world

Kyayam's legacy has unfolded.

Meraki

Creating is my passion

Inspiring the world is my ultimate mission,

What is the essence of thyself?

Transcendent,

A divergent is a world full of imitations

The Source is my Master

The Great Artist of all time.

Crossroads

She is at the crossroads of her path

A new frontier is within her grasp

The way to bring her Enlightenment is dawning,

As the promise of a bright tomorrow is approaching.

The Muse waits for Divine Providence

To find the answers her heart is seeking

She now sees the Light

Spreads her wings and vanished through the night.

Mutawaf Shaheed

Mutawaf Shaheed

C. E. Shy has been writing since the seventh grade. He continued writing through high school, until he became more involved in sports. After his graduation, he worked at the White Motors Company where he wrote for the company's newspaper. He started a column called: "The Poet's Corner." That was his first published work.

www.innerchildpress.com/c-e-shy.php

Omar or Umar

Words associated with windblown sands.
What shall my quill demand? Thoughts
that refresh oasis like an oasis. Thoughts
that eloped in her presence. To the heart
of mine that swells up like wells give up
water. Someone predicted you'd be there
in front of my stare. It has not been easy
to forget you.

When I sleep, I secretly weep on the pillow
you so readily abandoned. My mind drifts
hoping I'll find you. I'd rather search that sulk.
Inside me and all around me I still inhale your
fragrances. Why could you have not waited
maybe I could have blamed Satan?

I require your breath on my neck. Our hands
entwined making a fist that we can shake at a
world that tried to deny us. You ask why us?
Your kiss is our refrain. My memory will not
let you escape, unless I can escape with you.

Your nature was too rebellious to capture on
my canvas. Too many steps to retrace that
walked in our sandals, from dune to dune
until high noon. Under the date palm we sat
saying never ever always together. No need
to go home, I'd be there alone only with you
in my head.

Too Many So What's

Too many pieces to pick up, so what? Too many memories to unwind, only to become unwound. So many mistakes to unmake. Too many hearts to unbreak. Too many details not to be lying. Not enough time to rewind. Too many of my folks have been dying. Too many flickers not enough flames.

Too many sows running the pen, this an honor camp we're living in. Too many questions where there are no answers to rend. Too many wrongs to make right. Too many loop holes for it to be tight. So many lives lived in vain, so few ways to explain.

Every day the sun comes up, there is another demon that shows up. His purpose is just to lead you astray. When becoming conscience of such, there is too much vomit to throw up. Too many I's to dot, too many T's to cross, used to confuse your original thoughts.

Too many playing Russian roulette, with genetics to cover up some no name brand of cosmetics. Losing time playing tic- tack – toe. Too many, having dialogue with witches and devils, being convinced it is better to be on their level. Too many passwords have you disturbed.

Too many plotters planning plots with plotters to turn your sons into your daughter. Patting you on the back and saying to you, hey buddy, that's the way to go. You know what I'm telling is true. Too many sick bastards running the show. Not too many plans on how to make them go.

Mutawaf Shaheed

To all of them the people don't matter they are just cannon fodder. Some of them, the people, they had to spray along the way to keep them in line. Too many new magazines that are featuring new creatures, telling you the trend that's in, is you being like them. Freaks of nature leading the way for all those whose lives that are not safe.

Putting mink coats on frogs, shoes on dogs, doing lap dances with holy cows. Winding up in insane asylums and don't know how. Too many strange sounds all day long , making at least half of your decisions go all wrong. Mind twerks with jerks keeping your brain restrained.

Following trends with gender bends, so you can try to fit in. Too many creep thieves stealing your thoughts replacing them with theirs. Telling you that Santa Claus lives upstairs.
Locked in a chat box where you can't be found. I think what
you are dealing with is enough to be said . Still trying to wear
some-one else's shoes. Is that somebody under your bed?

Hey D, can you turn off the tape recorder aki? Ok, Thanks.

Try Passing By

All the people passing by ,faces graced
with smiles and sorrow. Some with
holding their dreams of tomorrow.
Wearing disguises of who they really
are. Rising , fading, wading through
the crowded passage ways as the eyes
say, they don't know. New footsteps
take the place of the one before. Lying
eyes take the spot where crying eyes
once cried.

Stopping, window shopping. A chance
glance might be the one that sticks.
Sidewalks accommodate crutches and
canes as traffic lights change. Always
aware of the pickpockets who gaze upon
the passer- by. In the midst of the crush
someone tries to advertise, hoping some-
body stops to listen, the others rush,
saying to themselves, don't want to hear
more lies.

The sounds
are indistinguishable. Inhaling different
odors,
rubbing shoulders in passing, coming in
contact
with complete strangers. Walking by those
who
cuss, while waiting on the bus that never
comes
on time. The old lady, just thought she saw
great

Mutawaf Shaheed

Scott. Someone dropped a coffee cup, a
homeless
guy picked up, looked inside then raised
his hands
in praise. A faint sound of the blues, I seem
to lose
as my pace goes up tempo.

I just missed an old friend who was in a hurry
passing the other way. Wow the familiar smell I
smell is coming from the roasted peanut store.
Hundreds of colors blend catching my attention
now and then, all mixed in are the drunk, the
deviants, demons and devils, pass by on the way
to who the hell knows where. Some people slow
down and stop, to open the door to the bar, some
even say, excuse me.

 A candy wrapper stuck on a dude's shoe, it really
wrinkling his smooth. The weather is wet and fifty-
five outside. Cell phones raised eye high. Little kid's
hand held by mommy dearest. She doesn't know
where his daddy is. Heading to her lawyer so she
will know what to do.

Buses, trucks and cars pass fast, faster that they
should. You too slow to say slow down! Delivery
truck blocking the cross walk, it starts moves when
you try to walk around. The people are on time or
early or late. A picturesque mess at best. Maybe I
could walk in the street? All I'm trying to do is just
pass right by.

hülya n. yılmaz

hülya n. yılmaz

Of Turkish descent, hülya n. yılmaz [sic] is Professor Emerita (Penn State, U.S.A.), Director of Editing Services (Inner Child Press International, U.S.A.), and a trilingual literary translator. Before her poetry and prose publications, she authored an extensive research book in German on cross-cultural literary influences.

Her works of literature include a trilingual collection of poems, memoirs in verse, prose poetry, short stories, a bilingual poetry book, and two books of poetry (one, co-authored). Her poetic offerings appeared in numerous anthologies of global endeavors.

hülya writes creatively to attain and nourish a comprehensive awareness for and development of our humanity.

hülya n. yılmaz, a traveler on the journey called "life" . . .

Writing Web Site
https://hulyanyilmaz.com/

Editing Web Site
https://hulyasfreelancing.com

Fill the Cup

"Oh, Saki*, fill the Cup!
Pour the Wine.
I am to wed the Divine,"

Omar Khayyam, the Lover, utters
in his intoxication with the Path*.

Drunk with the essence of the Beloved,
he falls into ecstasy.

"Join me in my rejoice,
for I was revived in Sama*.
Onto my doorstep came Baka*."

In Dhikr*, Khayyam utters again:
"Fill the cup. Fill the cup.
Fana* has neared our gate.
I am at last the dust at His feet."

Fill the Cup!
Fill the Cup!

*Saki: Wine bearer
The Path: the Sufis' much-quested way to Divine Love
Sufi: Muslim mystic
Sama: Listening
Dhikr: An Islamic prayer in repetition of Allah's different names
Baka: Life with, through, in, and for Allah
Fana: Dying into Allah

The Cloak

Don't judge me by the rough cloak I wear,
there is already much in this world
for all of us to bear.

Fill your heart with eternal love instead.
His dusty feet are where we return to bed.

On the Path to Divine Love,
we are one for once and for all.
Hear the chants of ecstasy nearing our hall.
Let's dance and lose the self in Sama.
Let's dissolve the self in Baka
and conceive eternally Fana.

Don't judge me by the rough cloak I wear,
there is already much in this world to bear.

Dust

All this dust I see

heeds the call of Divine Love.

Oh, Fana, come! Come!

Teresa E. Gallion

Teresa E. Gallion

Teresa E. Gallion was born in Shreveport, Louisiana and moved to Illinois at the age of 15. She completed her undergraduate training at the University of Illinois Chicago and received her master's degree in Psychology from Bowling Green State University in Ohio. She retired from New Mexico state government in 2012.

She moved to New Mexico in 1987. While writing sporadically for many years, in 1998 she started reading her work in the local Albuquerque poetry community. She has been a featured reader at local coffee houses, bookstores, art galleries, museums, libraries, Outpost Performance Space, the Route 66 Festival in 2001 and the State of Oklahoma's Poetry Festival in Cheyenne, Oklahoma in 2004. She occasionally hosts an open mic.

Teresa's work is published in numerous Journals and anthologies. She has two CDs: *On the Wings of the Wind* and *Poems from Chasing Light*. She has published three books: *Walking Sacred Ground, Contemplation in the High Desert* and *Chasing Light*.

Chasing Light was a finalist in the 2013 New Mexico/Arizona Book Awards.

The surreal high desert landscape and her personal spiritual journey influence the writing of this Albuquerque poet. When she is not writing, she is committed to hiking the enchanted landscapes of New Mexico. You may preview her work at

http://bit.ly/1aIVPNq or ***http://bit.ly/13IMLGh***

Teresa E. Gallion

The Genius of Omar

Mathematics, philosophy, astronomy, and poetry.
Now that is poetry stew at its best
rising from a genius and master of the word.

And the world only knows you, my friend,
for your poetry quatrains in the Rubaiyat.
Was that the influence of mathematics?

I wander, what impact philosophy
did to stimulate your blank page
while your Gemini twin gazed the stars?

No Matter Where

Everybody loves me.
But I have no need
to be loved by everybody.
I have a burning inside me
to be loved by you.

You cannot be pushed or pulled.
The hope vessel is docked
in the harbor.
Some day you may come to me.

I will reserve a space
in my love garden for you.
Even if I am no longer able
to respond,
that love seat will wait with
warmth for you.

I will slip on my joyful smile
whenever I hear your voice
no matter where I may be.

To the Awakened

Love floods all the boundaries
protecting me
and I am still blind.
Love floods all the sideroads
with light
and I still cannot not see.

I shut down.
Give my resignation
to two legged creatures,
stamped
humankind I resign.

Earth Mother rolls in tears for me.
I walk in her footprints
never ending my plea
for understanding.

She says, bend your knees 100 days,
then stand up. I comply.
Stand up and walk out of the forest.

I wear a sacred scarf,
armed in grace, ready
to offer love to all
who are awake.

Ashok K. Bhargava

Ashok K. Bhargava

ASHOK BHARGAVA is a poet, writer, inspirational speaker and a literary consultant. He has attended poetry conferences in Italy, Turkey, India and Philippines. His latest book "Riding the Tide" about his battle with cancer has been translated and published in Arabic, Hindi, Telugu and Bengali languages. He is a contributing writer to several anthologies worldwide including World Poetry Almanac 2014. He has been published in numerous print and online magazines.

Ashok has won many accolades including Poet Ambassador to Japan, Kalidasa International award, World Poetry Lifetime Achievement award, Writers Beyond Borders Peace award and Tapsilog Leadership award for his community involvement. He is founder of Writers International Network Canada Society to discover, nourish, recognize and celebrate writers, poets and artists and to assist them to network with the community at large. He is the author of eight books of poetry and one anthology. He is Artist-in-Residence at Moberly Arts & Cultural Centre and also co-edits the literary section of The Link Newspaper.

Quatrains of Omar

there is something so tender
about your tapestry of words,
each one different
like a clump of trees,
large and small, each with its own
life sustaining web of roots,
intricate and essential,
in harmony with the other shoots,
yet separate and distinct.

I could almost hear you oh Khayyam
reciting like a bird
hidden deep in the leafy trees,
spilling out rubaiyats.

they hum with a sound -
bees and birds,
flowers and leaves
as they wander around.

they thunder -
lightening clouds,
torrential rains
in amazing wonder.

they kiss -
lips on lips,
silent notes and
sweet rhymes.

they proclaim -
life is a gift
unwrap it
open it and use it.

Confused and Lost

you are no more lost
than them if you want

to love others and
be loved by them.

because something is
always amiss.

prepare the soil.
create the climate.

a seed must sprout
a flower must bloom

before a butterfly will
land to taste the nectar.

it is love
that we need

a taste of nectar
to nourish a seed.

* This poem verges on the spiritual dimension of human cravings to be loved by friends, relatives, lovers and strangers. Other than the physical experience of being loved, it is the mystic portals of the 'self-realization / felt reality' which is much more pleasurable than the mundane reality of the universe. It is the ephemerality of everything in life and beyond...

Metamorphosis

I am in
the melody of every song
sparkle of the sun rays
twinkle of the stars.

I am in
every smile you see
every hug you receive
every laugh you hear.

And I promise to be there
to reach out and
look out for you
because I love you.

what a caterpillar may call
the end of life
I call it
a colorful butterfly.

Caroline 'Ceri Naz' Nazareno Gabis

Caroline 'Ceri' Nazareno-Gabis

Caroline 'Ceri Naz' Nazareno-Gabis, author of Velvet Passions of Calibrated Quarks, World Poetry Canada International Director to Philippines is a multi-awarded poet, editor, journalist, educator, peace and women's advocate. She believes that learning other's language and culture is a doorway to wisdom.

Among her poetic belts include **Gabrielle Galloni Memorial Panorama International Youth Award** 2022, Panorama Youth Literary Awards 2020, 7th Prize Winner in the 19th, 20th and 21st Italian Award of Literary Festival; Writers International Network-Canada ''Amazing Poet 2015'', The Frang Bardhi Literary Prize 2014 (Albania), Poet Journalist Award 2014 (Tuzla, Istanbul, Turkey) and World Poetry Empowered Poet 2013 (Vancouver, Canada). She's a featured member of Association of Women's Rights and Development (AWID), The Poetry Posse, Galaktika Poetike, Asia Pacific Writers and Translators (APWT), Axlepino and Anacbanua. Her poetry and children's stories have been featured in different anthologies and magazines worldwide.

Links to her works:

http://panitikan.ph/2018/03/30/caroline-nazareno-gabis/

https://apwriters.org/author/ceri_naz/

http://www.aveviajera.org/nacionesunidasdelasletras/id1181.html

The Polymath's Equations

Under the map of stars

He writes equations

The binomial expansion

Turns my mathematical solutions

From cubic to astronomic calculations,

His words dwell in the codes

Of *Rubáiyát, a celebration of life!*

The litany of religious and political nuances,

His quatrains are far immeasurable,

Written for the humanity,

Underneath the bough.

Ode To The Family

I have myself, the simple scarlet on your vase
I asked for nothing, but you gave me life and sunshine
The smile, the hug, the cuddle, the care & the love
I am happy to the little things I have
You all give me light to complete my being
I am truly deeply thankful for all the arms
That make my wholeness back once more
You are the dream I dreamt and dreaming
To love, to cherish, to treasure
I love you so no matter what, no matter when
Until I know how to give up all, even my life.

When You Rise Up

If you trust you can do more today,

Heal yourself like a courageous beaver

And slowly, be the cheetah.

You are meant to mend the future's prophesy

From the ruins of palmistry,

Go and create hopeful lines

Of real foundations

Of life's miracles,

You are a rising ember

Entering the heaven's doors

Like a promise of renewal and resurgence.

Swapna Behera

Swapna Behera

Swapna Behera is a trilingual poet, translator, environmentalist, editor from India and author of seven books of different genres including one on children's literature on Environment. She is the recipient of International UGADI AWARD 2019, honoured from Gujurat Sahitya Akademi 2022, 2021 International Poesis Award of Honor as Jury, Pentasi B World Fellow Poet, Honoured Poet of India from Seychelles Government and International awards from Algeria, Morocco, Kajhakhstan, modern Arabic Literary Renaissance of Egypt, International Arts Council Argentina etc. Her stories, poems, articles are published in many International and National magazines and ezines. Her poem A NIGHT IN THE REFUGEE CAMP is translated into 67 languages. She has received over 60 National and International Awards. At present she is the Cultural Ambassador for India and South Asia of Inner Child and the life member of Odisha Environmental Society

Email
swapna.behera@gmail.com

Web Site
http://swapnabehera.in/

Omar Khayam ;The Astronomer Poet

Omar Khayyam a Persian polymath,
mathematician ,philosopher born in Nishapur
famous for his scientific achievements
the astronomer scientist poet of Persia
hundreds of quatrains he wrote
rubaiyat the pithy observation
on complex subjects such as love, death, God
the existence of contribution after life
"set not thy heart on any good or gain"
sky is the inverted bowl
Khayyam famous for classification
solution of cubic equation
by intersecting a parabola with a circle
designed the Jalali calendar
duration of solar year parallel axiom
his writings are
combination of nihilism ,fatalism, agnosticism
rubaiyat is a verse consisting of four line stanzas
he taught the court as a jurisprudence
the ultimate question of life and death
rubaiyat imparting an epicurean style of philosophy
the caravan of life is moving
a book of verses, a jug of wine, a loaf of bread now that is divine
thousand quatrains of rubaiyat
"there was a door to which I found no key
there was a veil past which I could not see "
Indeed heaven and hell are inside …

The Canvas Of Sand

sand is the big canvas
you can draw a house ,a horse ,
a plastic ban message or world cup foot ball
he is Sudarsan Pattanaik a sand artist from Odisha, India
a visionary and world record holder
recipient of Pdmashri ;India's fourth civilian Award
his concepts so unique when he constructs huge statues
his fingers worship the sand
sand has multiple textures, soft or coarse
polished or rough
sand sings in sync with the anthem of the sea
on the solitude of the sea shore
he imagines the concept
 impish waves may wash away after a couple of minutes
but can any one wash the creativity ?
it is printed in the brain and heart
sculptures are immortal
the mystical thoughts dance in tandem with the portrait
the artist sits and waits
celebrates the creativity
the world rejoiceswith him
he is Sudarsan Pattanaik a global sand artist
beyond boundaries.

Biryani vs Ragi Balls

His Highness ordered for the best biryani
best rice with goat legs, lot of spices
saffron, cardamom, cinnamon sticks. cashew and raisin
rose water, mint and the list goes on and on
of course fried onions added to the juicy rice
the fragrance spread far and wide
the chef arranged the table with colourful biryani
the skill test of the chef
the taste buds of the ministers sizzle
affluent they all were
just behind the palace a poor shepherd
came back from the jungle with his sheep and goat
sad he was as he lost a goat, the healthiest one
his wife cooked ragi balls in the open air
that they grew in that hillock
the grand banquet was over with wine and music
in the silent night tears of the shepherd merged with ragi balls
for he lost a goat whose bleat echoed in his ear
pieces of the goat in the biryani
each piece crying for its master
two drops of tears soaked the ragi balls in the thatched house
his highness was amazed to taste the new dish
so he rewarded the chef with the hillock that grew ragi and the sheep
but was awake whole night
as it was tough to digest the high voltage spices
the chef was happy to get the reward of that hillock and all the sheep was his

for he needed meat to make the biryani frequently
the shepherd lost ;the chef received
salty ragi balls understand the language of animals
that the biryani can never …….

(Biryani is a mixed rice dish with meat and spices that is originated from Iran
ragi is commonly called finger millet and one type of staple diet in farming communities)

Swapna Behera

Albert 'Infinite' Carrasco

Albert 'Infinite' Carassco

Albert "Infinite The Poet" Carrasco is an urban poet, mentor and public speaker.

Albert believes his experience of growing up in poverty, dealing with drugs and witnessing murder over and over were lessons learnt, in order to gain knowledge to teach. Albert's harsh reality and honesty is a powerfully packed punch delivered through rhyme. Infinite grew up in the east part of the Bronx and still resides there, so he knows many young men will follow the same dark path he followed looking for change. The life of crime should never be an option to being poor but it is, very often.

Infinite poetry @lulu.com

Alcarrasco2 on YouTube

Infinite the poet on reverbnation

Infinite Poetry

www.lulu.com/us/en/shop/al-infinite-carrasco/infinite-poetry/paperback/product-21040240.html

www.innerchildpress.com/albert-carrasco

Omar Khayyam

I am Persian, born in Nishapur. mathematics, astronomy, philosophy and poetry are a few of my passions. My contributions to the above was made during the Seljuk dynasty during the first crusade. As a mathematician I'm notable for classification and solutions of cubic equations, I provided geometric solutions by the intersection of Conics and also contributed to the understanding of the parallel axiom. As an astronomer I also used math to calculate the duration of a solar year with precision. Doing so, I created a solar calendar called the Jalali calendar which provided the basis for the Persian calendar that is still in use after nearly a millennium. I am also a philosopher, a student of Ibn Sina, known in the west as Avicenna, when it came to early medicine, Avicenna was considered the father. To me there is no religious sect, I believe in Agnosticism and pessimism. My life's journey and visions can also be read through my works of poetry.

The clouds

those clouds followed me, it rained blood rain, each drop had a name, John dropped Jane dropped through the rain drops if you didn't know the name of those rain drops. I've seen the ones I ran and reigned with in the game names drop, i saw my fathers name for crying out loud, drop from a crying cloud up top. rain drop pain dropped from a cloud that ceased to clot, please stop the rain, I can't walk without stepping on a stain.through time the cloud got more dense, hence thicker blood drops to commence, thunder storms and lightning poured out phlebotomy, the cloud that killed the monotony, of forming a monopoly followed me continually dropping blood that leaked from my friends, foes and family.

Rain drops kept falling from the dead onto my head, I didn't wipe them, because then it would be like I got caught red handed, like I was the cause of a murder case, so instead, I let the murder drip down my face.

When I went indoors then cloud hovered over my residence, the blood drops fell on my awning sounding like a snare drum beat of ghetto pestilence, when I sleep it dissipates, But as soon as I wake in the morning, my first sight out the window is that damn cloud forming.

Don't go

Many men didn't want me to retire and raise my kids, that didn't suit em, that wasn't detrimental to their income, they wanted me to keep raising my children sauer along with smith and wesson for protection, it was beneficial to them if I stood in the hood buss'n mine and Chopin cookies to nickels and dimes. Ayo Inf I need about a six month run, I need you to hold me down in these trapped up slums, take a block by swingn that shit like a sword, let me and my team live and we'll pay you rent like a landlord, ayo inf can I get a shift, they needed money drip and godfather spliffs. I let em all eat, I wasn't turning my back on anyone, if I win we all won, plus I knew how hard it was to come up in these BX streets. I put that time in, put that work in, in the hood and the kitchen, I went through it all, got caked up, hit up, locked up, fell and came back up, plus, I buried most of the men with whom I came up. There was nothing left to witness but my own death, so I left before soul theft.

Michelle
Joan
Barulich

Michelle Joan Barulich

Michelle Joan Barulich was born in Honolulu, Hawaii on the island of Oahu. She started writing poetry and songs with her younger brother Paul. They have written many songs in their teen years. She is currently studying Alternative Medicine and would like to become a Homeopathic Doctor. Michelle loves all kinds of animals and birds; she does wild rehabilitation. She has also rescued rock pigeons that make great pets.

https://www.facebook.com/michelle.barulich

Seize the Secret

Omar, thank you for your contributions.

To mathematics, astronomy, philosophy, and poetry

Leading the way as an astronomer

With precision and accuracy

You designed the jalai calendar

Which is still in use to this day

You were unequalled

In scientic knowledge and many in your day

Called you the epithet of the wise.

Obstacle

I need warmth and security
I feel fire surrounding me
The sky endless like my grief
And clouds their weeping just like me
Can anyone hear their scream
So loud across the world
An echo never to be heard
Is this the world we have made?
We walk among hells corridors
Looking for any site of light
We touch death so many times
Again, once more we kill the crimes
Can anyone hear their scream
So loud across the world
An echo never to be heard
Is this the world we have made?

Song

Your song has lifted me up

Up from the tunnel

The spirit of the words has melted my heart

All the lines you sing, I feel

You touched my soul, in so many different ways

Visions of you, I see blue

And where there are shadows you are there

The song, music of the night made my spirit soar

And my soul began to take flight

Help me make the music of the night,,,

Eliza
Segiet

Eliza Segiet

Eliza Segiet graduated with a Master's Degree in Philosophy at Jagiellonian University.

Received *Global Literature Guardian Award* – from Motivational Strips, World Nations Writers Union and Union Hispanomundial De Escritores (UHE) 2018.

Nominated for the Pushcart Prize 2019, 2021.

Laureate *Naji Naaman Literary Prize 2020,*

International Award Paragon of Hope (2020),

World Award 2020 *Cesar Vallejo* for Literary Excellence. Laureate of the Special Jury *Sahitto International Award* 2021, World Award *Premiul Fănuș Neagu* 2021.

Finalist *Golden Aster Book* World Literary Prize 2020, *Mili Dueli* 2022, Voci nel deserto 2022.

At the international Festival of Poetry CAMPIONATO MONDIALE DI POESIA (2021/2022) she won the title of vice-champion of the world.

Award BHARAT RATNA RABINDRANATH TAGORE INTERNATIONAL AWARD (2022).

Award - *World Poets Association* (2023).

Laureate Between words and infinity *"International Literary Award (2023).*

Eliza Segiet

The Bitter Taste of Existence
In memory of Omar Khayyama*

His immortal words make
mortal man realise
that for centuries
the world has been immersed in questions
about the nature of existence.

From the sweetness of words
to bitter conclusions,
he has given insight into the past
in relation to the present.
The collected notes of life
and the fear of death reveal
the bitter taste of existence.

Will anything remain
when the grave
towers over the body?

He did not believe in the existence of
invisible powers.

Confusion, anxiety, uncertainty
formed a pillar of thought of his reality,
his questioning of eternity
and the certainty of the impermanence of everything.

* Omar Khayyam - Persian politician known for his contributions to mathematics, astronomy, philosophy and poetry.

Translated by Dorota Stępińska

With the Siren

She still cannot believe it.
that the world available to her now
– is an open window and emptiness.
She bares her experiences
to herself.

The neighbor is not very interested
in her fate,
a bystander will not see
imprisoned on the sixth floor
solitude.
Known and unknown,
now it is like the air.

Only when they arrive for her with the siren,
whispers are heard through the leaky door:
– *She's still alive. She's so fatigued.*

It is a pity that when she needed bread,
no one heard her hunger.

Translated by Artur Komoter

Normality

We become indifferent
to the human next to us.
We do not notice
that someone
only pretends to be strong.

With pockets full of
unfinished business,
desires and uncertainties,
maybe we also often
wear masks?

With hope we expect
that we will not be alone,

we look out for
– normality
in abnormality.

Translated by Artur Komoter

William S. Peters Sr.

William S. Peters, Sr.

Bill's writing career spans a period of over 50 years. Being first Published in 1972, Bill has since went on to Author in excess of 50 additional Volumes of Poetry, Short Stories, etc., expressing his thoughts on matters of the Heart, Spirit, Consciousness and Humanity. His primary focus is that of Love, Peace and Understanding!

Bill says . . .

I have always likened Life to that of a Garden. So, for me, Life is simply about the Seeds we Sow and Nourish. All things we "Think and Do", will "Be" Cause and eventually manifest itself to being an "Effect" within our own personal "Existences" and "Experiences" . . . whether it be Fruit, Flowers, Weeds or Barren Landscapes! Bill highly regards the Fruits of his Labor and wishes that everyone would thus go on to plant "Lovely" Seeds on "Good Ground" in their own Gardens of Life!

to connect with Bill, he is all things Inner Child

www.iaminnerchild.com

Personal Web Site

www.iamjustbill.com

Khayyam

Oh how I love the sound of the name . . .
I thought it to be poetic when I first
Became aware,
And 'lo and behold'
My endearment became a stronghold
In the lyrics of "Persian-ality"

Khayyam, Hafiz, Rumi . . .
Quite the family

So I did as he said
With my life
Because of those immortalized words
'eat drink and be merry'

I thank you brother Omar
For you lyricism . . .

Khayyam my personal Rubaiyat . . .

Life is for Living

We spend our entire lives dying,
Lying to ourselves
While vying for unattainable fruits

We dream of such things
As legacy, memories and 'what ifs'
.....
Yet the journey into oblivion
Continues

Shall you remember these acquired lessons
Next lifetime?
The fruitful and fruitless,
The thoughts that have no seed.

Does the soul grow,
Or is its compacity
Already fulfilled

There is the infinite
And the eternal,
But ..
What does that mean to me
If I can not let go
Of this small thing
I imagined my 'self'
To be ...
Or not to be?

The words of Ovid
Strike a resonant chord
Somewhere in my seemingly
Unexplored depths ...

William S. Peters, Sr.

"Vivam!" "I will live.",
After all,
Is not Life for Living?

Somewhere in the darkness
I have contemplated this acute light
And the dawning of its truth,
And my soul yet still yearns
To reconcile with its purpose.

Life is for Living .... so do so!

The Short Nap

If one were to consider
The concept of eternity,
We would have to admit
That this existence we call life
Is but a blink of the 'Cosmic Eye'

We spend most of our lives
Attempting to define ourselves
Making futile attempts
To affirm the baseless imaginings
Of our divine grandeur

In this thick soup of this quasi-reality,
We over-season the weak affirmations
Of our adopted and borrowed realities

Sometimes the meal is palatable,
Some times bitter,
Most times non-descript

Theere is a prevailing vagueness
That we rail against
In our supposed 'wakening',
But truth be told
We are mostly
Sleeping our way through
This brief journey

We connect the moments
And store them in the deep recesses
Of memories
To be visited
From time to time

William S. Peters, Sr.

Worry not,
For the time for sleep
Pales in the face of
The eternal and the infinite...
How do I know? ...
Simple,
This is not the first time
I took a short nap

February 2024 Featured Poets

Caroline Laurent Turunç

Julio Pavanetti

Lidia Chiarelli

Lina Buividavičiūtė

Caroline Laurent Turunç

Caroline Laurent Turunç

Caroline LAURENT Turunç is from Antakya, Turkey, from Arab origin, she is the daughter of a family of nine children. She has a sociology degree and has written over 1500 poems since 2013, received many certificates from abroad, and participated in nearly 60 local and foreign anthologies. Her poems are still published in many international journals and websites. She is writing a novel that she is about to finish. She published two collections of poems, "Between the Orient and the North" and "Desert Lily". He came second among 2575 poets from each country at the world literature championship held in Romania. She won an award at the eighth spring poetry festival held in the town of Yan, China, causing it to be selected for the "World Poet Literary Museum" commissioned by the Silk Road Cultural Center of Northwest University of China.

The Earth Has Split!

The earth has split and I saw myself falling into the pensive waters of the rivers.
The fresh waters of the rebel river swept the tired walls of an unfortunate city, frayed fate and memories flowed into deep scarred rivers.

Between the cries of the crowd, my heart was crushed by the pure and cold smell of the sun
I ascended to ancient times.

I wish my ears were deafened by the harshness of the east and the cries of the north wind.

Maybe I wouldn't have felt the acrid smell of my red soil in Damas.

In the rage of the deep blue sea of the Mediterranean, I wouldn't hear the hum of the seashells drifting to the beach with the sands, the cries of pain.

O creator of the bluebirds of Babylon, give me more than a pure, unused gift.

The tower of silence ascended to the seven heavens
My roots are the oldest soil.
I want to go back to where I am
I want to go back to the deepest scarred parts of the mind.

I want to return to the arms of existence.

I really don't know if I can live or not
I promise not to be angry with you and my destiny, if I fail
I will bury myself in the stars, the moon, the sun, the flowing rocks or the transparent pebbles.

The Year of the Poet XI ~ February 2024

Pancasila

It is the national ideology of Indonesia.
Pancasila means five principles.
These five principles, which cannot be considered independently of each other, are as follows:
1. Monotheism.
2. A just and modern society.
3. Indonesia's unity.
4. Democracy.
5. Social justice

This Indonesia-based reform movement has become a reference for the Indonesian people to fight against the conservatives, and they have achieved successful results thanks to this reform.

****
****

pancasila
- Kamer, the black diamond that illuminates the darkness of the night, the silver that illuminates the morning

When slapped, it doesn't just fall to the ground -
Its beauty, grace and richness are endless.
Don't think you can knock him down and never get up again.
Of course he gets up, of course he comes back, gets up and does whatever he says.

The figure of that morning "
The warm heat of that cold air
The blood value of that land
Don't call him pale, don't call him pale.
root of that banyan tree

Remember, the right word is much heavier than a slap and a gun.

Don't make me open my mouth, don't ask me that, I know he's bad and what his intentions are.
- Don't tell me what half a million saplings are.
You are the ignorant of the ignorant, if every flower was a flower, the world would be a flower

No to moral cruelty, no to tolerance of the ignorant-
don't try to surprise me

So it looks like you're firing me

Pancasila - I'm not firing you, you'll go yourself. Privacy, darkness, dimness, uncertainty will never be an obstacle for those who want to step into the light.

Dreams Have Turned Brown!

O verses of wounds, ashes and silence,
The ditches overflow, the trees where the birds are placed
in the gardens of the century hang down,
The pride of the world darkens like shabby stones.

from North to south,
fragile thorns of grass spread around
The fold of the earth is slowly shaking !
Heavy clouds gather towards the mountains, the slopes
begin to slip reluctantly.
And you sit there like an arrogant sultan

Tell me, tell me how spring will come with this arrogance
How will souls dance if everything changes?
A long vibrating frenzy will mourn the discord of the
worlds

We don't know who beat who, who loves who.
Desert migration from everywhere instills its naked
conquest,
Those who have nothing to give
kisses a stained glass window with a herd of transmitted
miracles.

oh if my eyes were blind oh if my eyes were blind
If I sit forever under the root of an old tree like a cathedral
And then if I rot like a worthless leaf out of my rib cage
My heart longs for victory, if it destroys everything like a
flood and starts again

Now my broken veins are dripping from my eye socket
my starry skin can't even bear the fruit of alchemy
insect law in my chest,

Caroline Laurent Turunç

It creates a burning sensation in the hands,
and slowly kill the thorns on me.

Ah, the stars in the resin of my race, a brutality in my bones
As if trying to break the harpsichord of the ages, a pain in
my chest prevents me from being reborn.

Julio Pavanetti

Julio Pavanetti

Julio Pavanetti
(Montevideo, Uruguay, 1954)

He is a poet living in Benidorm, Spain. Director of the International Poet's Association "Liceo Poético de Benidorm". Associate Academic and Honorary Member of the North American Academy of Modern Literature. Director of the poetry collection "Azul" of Enkuadres Publishers, Spain. Director of the Benidorm International Poetry Festival. Member of the Association of Spanish Writers and Artists. Member of the Spanish Collegiate Association of Writers. Titular member of the Tomitana Academy (Romania). He has published twelve poetry books, one of them, "The spiral of time" in Romanian/Spanish bilingual edition, published in Bucharest, Romania in 2012. His book "At the touch of a silent flesh", won the first prize in the contest of Aspe, Spain, in 2015, and was published in 2018 in English/Spanish bilingual edition. His book "Mërgimi Dhemb" (Exile hurts) was published in 2021 in Albania and Kosovo in Albanian language. His book "Battute d'arresto" was published in Italy in Italian language in 2022 and the book won the prize of excellence for the book written in Italian by a foreign author, Rome, Italy, 2023. He had received many awards and recognitions, both for his poetry as for his cultural work. In 2021 he received the Award of Excellence for his Career in Rome, Italy, and won the 1st prize for foreign poets of the VIII Edition of the "Città del Galateo - Antonio De Ferraris" International Excellence Award, Rome, Italy. In February 2023 he received the Honorary Prize for the poet of the year 2023 awarded by the International Writers Association "Pjetër Bogdani" based in Brussels (Belgium) and Prishtina (Kosovo). He has participated in several poetry festivals and took part in more than 100 international anthologies. Many of his poems have been translated into 27 languages and have been published on innumerable international literary magazines.

The Embrace

We all wandered
without knowing the right path,
motionless in the midst of death
and of ourselves,
without coming to recognize their cards,
apart from the infinite breath.
Until a cold and sad June arrived.
They trampled on our illusions,
murdered our rebelliousness
and our references,
those that they -alienated
from their black poverty-
turned into immortals.

With our hair shorter,
we still sprout
like the moss that is born
between the cobblestones.
We went entwining
like ivy clings
to the peeling walls,
until we felt the heartbeat
of a strong and long embrace
that was sealed marenmedio (*)

* Marenmedio, that means "in the middle of the sea", is a word used by Juan Ramón Jiménez in the third fragment of his poem "Space" (Espacio)

Marenmedio
Or the inevitable influence of the waves

"What I have is in the middle of the waves…"
~ **Pablo Neruda**

"…And then, marenmedio, sea, more sea, eternal sea, with its eternal moon and sun for naked, as I, for naked, eternal…"
~ **Juan Ramón Jiménez**

In the middle of the waves
two oscillating tongues,
different, equal,
petals of a nocturnal rose
that end up folding,
to mate in the belly
of a bound sea.

In the middle of the waves,
between distant and distinct beaches
but moist with salt,
my two voices navigate:
sprightly, the one from the 20th century;
musty, the one from this century.
Exposed to the sun, they dry out…
Both are mine.

In the middle of the waves
I observe the journey,
permanent transit to nowhere.
I leave that shore
to bleed to death in sunsets
and enter the here and vice versa.

Julio Pavanetti

An ineffective cry
that the intestines of the sea
ooze of mortal invalidity.

We cannot run away from what we are.
Evolution or involution?

In the middle of the waves
I pass from twilight to dawn,
I see the fish jump that mock
every tear of yesterday,
however, they walk like imps
foaming my resistance,
and leaving me with the embers
that remain in my dreams
on the other side of the docks,
reviving me among the verses,
after the rain, but before oblivion.

In the middle of the waves,
subject to the whims
of their ups and downs,
I wait like an absent one,
supporting my solitude.
I dive in the dark
between exiles and homecoming,
I migrate to the warmth of memories,
and again, I return migration,
when the sun freezes
in the silence of the ocean.

In the middle of the waves
and sedimented in its sediment,
everything that I have is found
and everything that I lost,
they took in my troubles
and they took in my verses.

There remained my youth,
my father, my friends,
my mother, my memories,
my story that could not be,
this present and the future,
my heart full of horizons
long, unattainable,
shared among suns
and among a thousand warm moons,
there are my free dreams,
and my song, and my accent.

To what incomplete and indifferent shore,
to what mysterious stone altars,
to what piece of death do I belong?

The world still unsolved,
with bridges destroyed
by the inevitable influence
that the waves exert.
In the middle of the current
the cards fell,
but I remain on the road
even if everything remained *marenmedio…* (*)

* *Marenmedio, that means "in the middle of the sea", is a word used by Juan Ramón Jiménez in the third fragment of his poem "Space" (Espacio)*

Julio Pavanetti

Sadness

Sadness is... that dead time
without the spiral drawings
that smoke produces in the air;
it is dreams of the future
of a sleeping past
floating behind the screen
of worn-out memory.

Sadness is... the sense of guilt
as heavy as a slab.
It is the knife that is stuck
of falsehood, betrayal and deceit.

Sadness is... that feeling
of silent monologue
surrounded by loneliness.

It is the cauldron where they boil
chimeras and illusions;
it is an inventory of names
and lost memories
on the distant horizon,
it is a longing for childhood
and faded adolescence.

Sadness is... unmade sheets
but without smells or traces.
It is to feel always a stranger,
even in our own land
when returning from exile.

It is the shadow that our loves and memories left us,
nights with eyes open
linking the discomforts,
and inventing some futures

that will never come.

Sadness is... lack of projects,
and gradual aging.

It is a warehouse of silent screams,
powerlessness in the face of distance,
incomprehension and forgetfulness.

Sadness is... loneliness
               that remain completely alone.

We swim across the seas and climb the mountains
Though it is unbearably hot or cold or it heavily rains .
We don't return back, ahead we go
Though the strong winds blow.

Though we are hungry and thirsty ,
We move forward patiently.
We move on thorns that come in our way
We never step back but move forward night and day.

It's the Passion that helps us to win our race
Though many difficulties we face.
So ,until Passion in us plays its role
We can't achieve our desired goal.

Julio Pavanetti

Lidia Chiarelli

Lidia Chiarelli

Lidia Chiarelli is one of the Charter Members of Immagine & Poesia, the art literary Movement founded in Torino (Italy) in 2007 with Aeronwy Thomas. Installation artist and collagist. Coordinator of #DylanDay in Italy. She has become an award-winning poet since 2011 and she was awarded a Certificate of Appreciation from The First International Poetry Festival of Swansea (U.K.) for her broadside poetry and art contribution. Awarded with the Literary Arts Medal – New York 2020. Six Pushcart Prize (USA) nominations. Grand Jury Prize at Sahitto International Award 2021. In 2014 she started an inter-cultural project with Canadian writer and editor Huguette Bertrand publishing E Books of Poetry and Art online. Poetry Star, China 2022. Winner of KEL 2022. Her writing has been translated into30 languages and published in more than 150 Poetry magazines, and on web-sites in many countries.

https://lidiachiarelli.jimdofree.com/
https://lidiachiarelliart.jimdofree.com/
https://immaginepoesia.jimdofree.com/

Lidia Chiarelli

Water Prayer

to Dylan, Son of the Sea

Seagulls and restless rooks
challenge the wind
on this winter morning.

Under a pearl sky
the waves sing the rising sun -
the first glimpse of light on the horizon
   fades too soon.

Here and now
Dylan's words resound:
The waters of the heart
push in their tides…*

And from the ancient cliff
I pause and listen to
the voice of the sea:

a water prayer

that softly evaporates
among the fleeing clouds.

from: Light breaks where no sun shines

My liquid world
(amid winds of war)
to Dylan Thomas

This ashen day in March
opens with dancing shadows -
images carved in the air
of the Spring still too far.
An insidious mist enshrouds me in crescendo.
Among echoes in subtle vibration
teach me, Dylan, to take shelter in
my liquid world

teach me to feel the pulse
of the tides that ceaselessly
ebb and flow

And while time and space dissolve
in the primordial roar of the ocean

teach me to fly away, with you, from
the void ... of this bewilderment of that insanity*

* from: *Although through my bewildered way*

Lidia Chiarelli

Where Beauty dwells

Beauty dwells
in the splendor of a dawn
fading too soon.
Or in crimson and gold sunsets.

Beauty dwells
in the sun rays
that painters carry on canvas:

perfect pulses of energy
rapid and fatal touches
meant to stop the fleeting moment

in a glow of unutterable
light.

Lina

Buividavičiūtė

Lina Buividavičiūtė

Lina Buividavičiūtė was born on May 14, 1986. She is a poet and literary critic. Lina is an author of two poetry books in Lithuanian language. Her poetry is published in "Matter", "Masters", "Proverse poetry prize" contest anthologies, "Drunk monkeys", "Beyond words", "The Dewdrop", "Sad girls club", "The limit experience", "Beyond queer words", "Maudlin House", "Cathexis northwest press", "Red noise collective", "Poetry online" magazines and "Versopolis" poetry platform. Upcoming publications will appear in "New millennium writings", "Cathexis northwest press", "Red noise collective", „Box", „Sad girls club" and "Beyond words" magazines. These poems are translated from Lithuanian to English by Irma Šlekytė.

Lina Buividavičiūtė

A Letter to My Child of War

Oh child of mine, they say, when boys are born
for the whole generation – the war is upon us.
We birthed our sons around that time –
we rejoiced, matriarchs of the family,
but dark shapes loomed,
there was no peace. My grandmother had
already seen those shapes, before the Second
World War, she saw the sign of the cross
in the sky, women, solitudinous,
hauling on their shoulders all the yokes
of the world. On September 11
you'll turn eighteen, so I keep anxiously
glancing at the sky, following
the news from neighboring lands.

And yet I forgive you for being born, the child of war.

I can't begin to tell you, how much I wish
never to mark in lamb's blood
the door of our home upon your return.
I fervently hope you'll never know,
how much it weighs down my hands and heart,
the chill of the steel, when sweat breaks out
on sleepless nights as I count
those fallen. Is this hope meant
for you, or for me?

Still, what frightens the most aren't the stumps,
the phantoms of limbs, or the hair that's gone white –

but to never escape
the barren wind ghosts, and that nothing will be
as it was.

And yet I let you go, my child of war –
my reins can't hold back the steeds any longer.

The Dark Ages

For my son, for all travelers'
There's so much beauty it takes my breath away,
but in the evenings I talk to myself in my mind,
I say it's not too bad, it's all bearable,
it'll all wash off in the salty water,
I tell myself I'll climb atop one or two fortresses,
I'll have a couple of glasses of Sardinian wine,
I'll sail by some mysterious sea caves and be free;
my dark ages will pass without having properly begun,
that's what I tell myself at night, before the flamingos start singing,
that's how I rage when my three-year-old son does not see the beauty, then the clouds of sadness gather – he wants home,
back to his kittens, so I rise like a storm: why do you not want to see the vast world, why do you need that
damn triad – safety, consistency and a calm mother?
What do I need? What do I lack? We told everyone we travel together, we want our boy to see the world, Italian winds
and mountains, and us, away from daily routines, washed up on a new shore.
It's not you I wanted to show the world to, it's myself, so that
my dark ages would go by, but I never escaped them having realized –
when I give to you, I rob myself.

Apathy (the Weight of one's Hand)

I've never seen it raising a revolver, ready for
a slap of betrayal. I've never witnessed it tossing soil
on a three-year old's coffin, caressing an unloved one,
writing
the last letter, holding a hand of the one who's departing.
So, they say,
I have no right to gather so much heaviness in my elbows
and
forearms. I have no right, they say, to not move my wrist
bones.

I know I have to move these arms for the sake of the
bedridden,
for those marked with age spots, for those who've lost
everything,
for those whose limbs were torn off by shrapnel.

Hanging off the edge of the bed, on a frayed bedsheet,
despite
all the scolding, persuading, ultimatums, I cannot stroke my
child's head –
my hand grows heavy, because, I believe, as soon as I
touch him, the soil
  will start pouring onto him.

I fight using different shapes of blackness, with no blood
flowing to the ten
little fingers,
but if I'm called, if we once again need to stand hand in
hand, I promise you world
my hand,
for a short respite from an unworldly heaviness.

Lina Buividavičiūtė

Translated from Lithuanian by Irma Šlekytė

Remembering

our fallen soldiers of verse

Janet Perkins Caldwell
February 14, 1959 ~ September 20, 2016

Alan W. Jankowski
16 March 1961 ~ 10 March 2017

The Butterfly Effect

"IS" in effect

Inner Child Press

News

Published Books

by

Poetry Posse Members

We are so excited to share and announce a few of the current books, as well as the new and upcoming books of some of our Poetry Posse authors.

On the following pages we present to you ...

Inner Child Press News

Alicja Maria Kuberska
Jackie Davis Allen
Gail Weston Shazor
hülya n. yılmaz
Nizar Sartawi
Elizabeth E. Castillo
Faleeha Hassan
Fahredin Shehu
Kimberly Burnham
Caroline 'Ceri' Nazareno
Eliza Segiet
Teresa E. Gallion
William S. Peters, Sr.

Now Available

www.innerchildpress.com

The Year of the Poet XI ~ February 2024

Now Available
www.innerchildpress.com

Inner Child Press News

Now Available
www.innerchildpress.com

The Year of the Poet XI ~ February 2024

Now Available
www.innerchildpress.com

Inner Child Press News

Now Available
www.innerchildpress.com

The Year of the Poet XI ~ February 2024

Now Available
www.innerchildpress.com

Inner Child Press News

Now Available
www.innerchildpress.com

The Year of the Poet XI ~ February 2024

Now Available
www.innerchildpress.com

Inner Child Press News

Now Available at
www.amazon.com/gp/product/B08MYL5B7S/ref=
dbs_a_def_rwt_hsch_vapi_tkin_p1_i2

The Year of the Poet XI ~ February 2024

Now Available at
www.innerchildpress.com

Inner Child Press News

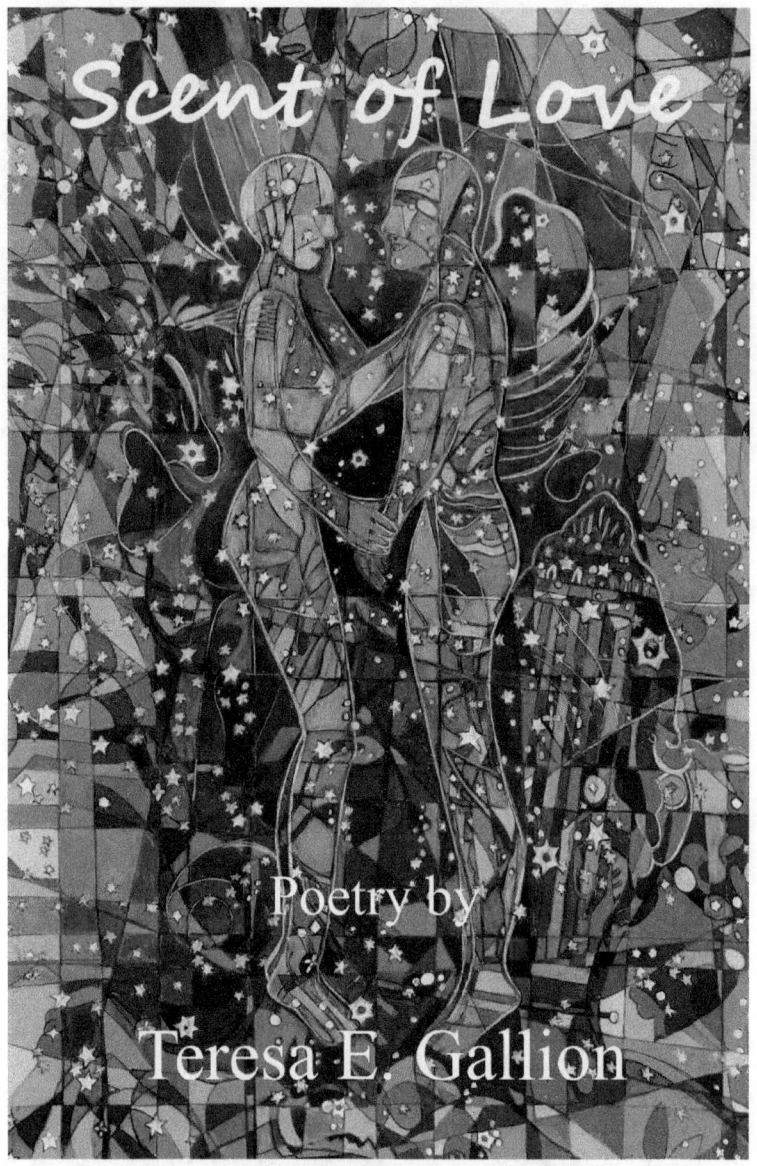

Now Available
www.innerchildpress.com

The Year of the Poet XI ~ February 2024

Now Available
www.innerchildpress.com

Inner Child Press News

Now Available
www.innerchildpress.com

The Year of the Poet XI ~ February 2024

Now Available
www.innerchildpress.com

Now Available
www.innerchildpress.com

The Year of the Poet XI ~ February 2024

The Book of krisar
volume v

william s. peters, sr.

Now Available
www.innerchildpress.com

Inner Child Press News

The Book of krisar
Volume I

william s. peters, sr.

The Book of krisar
Volume II

william s. peters, sr.

Now Available
www.innerchildpress.com

The Year of the Poet XI ~ February 2024

The Book of krisar
Volume III

william s. peters, sr.

The Book of krisar
Volume IV

william s. peters, sr.

Now Available
www.innerchildpress.com

Inner Child Press News

Now Available
www.innerchildpress.com

The Year of the Poet XI ~ February 2024

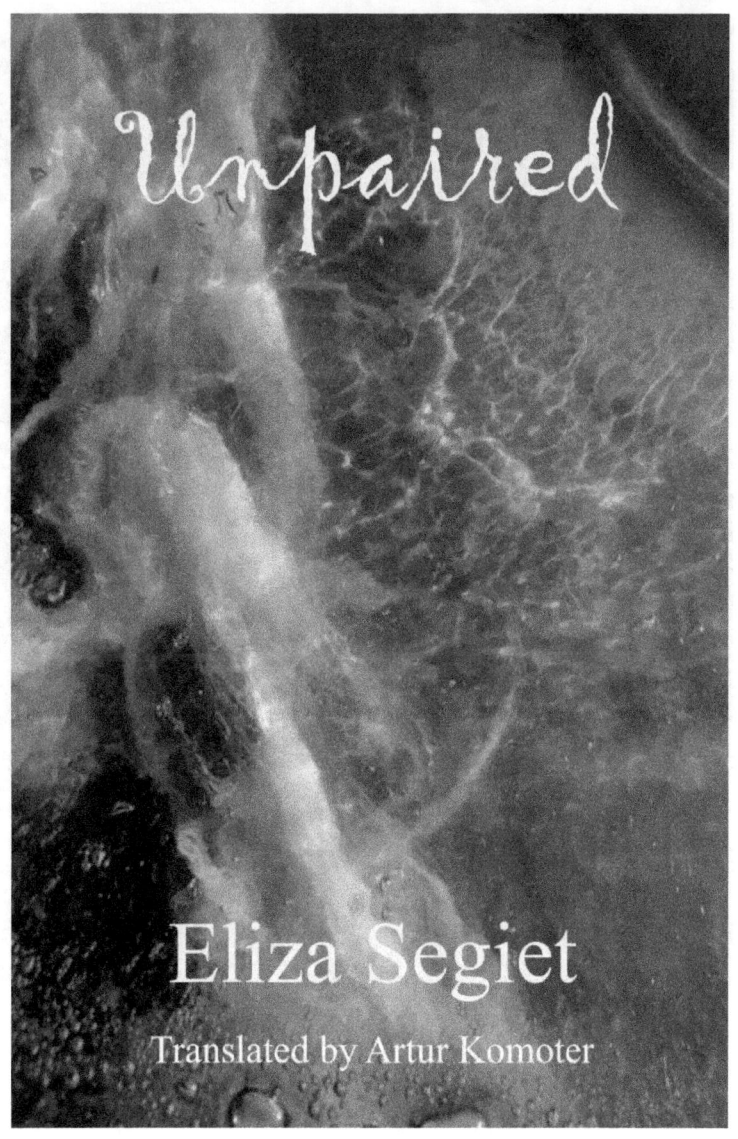

Private Issue
www.innerchildpress.com

Inner Child Press News

Now Available
www.innerchildpress.com

The Year of the Poet XI ~ February 2024

Now Available at
www.innerchildpress.com

Inner Child Press News

No Illusions
Through the Looking Glass

Jackie Davis Allen

Now Available at
www.innerchildpress.com

The Year of the Poet XI ~ February 2024

Now Available at
www.innerchildpress.com

Now Available at
www.innerchildpress.com

The Year of the Poet XI ~ February 2024

HERENOW

FAHREDIN SHEHU

Now Available at
www.innerchildpress.com

Inner Child Press News

Now Available at
www.innerchildpress.com

The Year of the Poet XI ~ February 2024

Now Available at
www.innerchildpress.com

Inner Child Press News

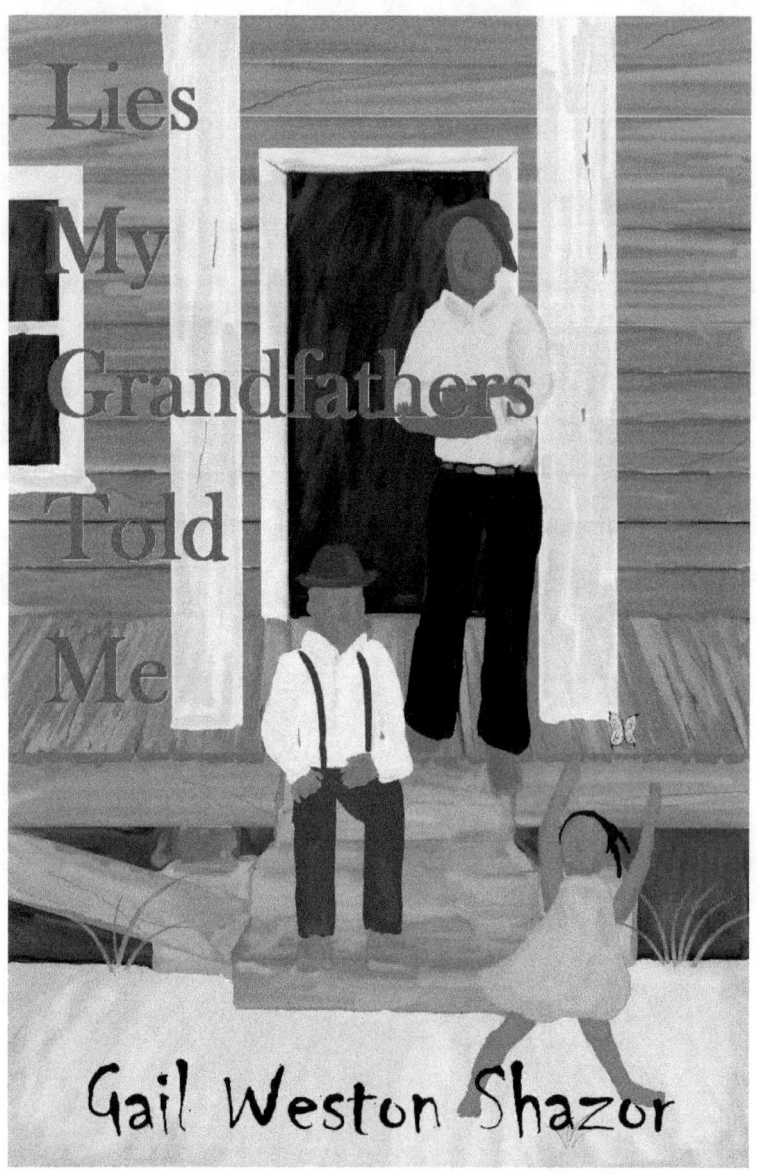

Now Available at
www.innerchildpress.com

The Year of the Poet XI ~ February 2024

Now Available at
www.innerchildpress.com

Inner Child Press News

Now Available at
www.innerchildpress.com

The Year of the Poet XI ~ February 2024

Now Available at
www.innerchildpress.com

Inner Child Press News

Now Available at
www.innerchildpress.com

The Year of the Poet XI ~ February 2024

Now Available at
www.innerchildpress.com

Inner Child Press News

Now Available at
www.innerchildpress.com

The Year of the Poet XI ~ February 2024

Other Anthological works from

Inner Child Press International

www.innerchildpress.com

Inner Child Press Anthologies

Now Available
www.worldhealingworldpeacepoetry.com

Inner Child Press Anthologies

Now Available
www.worldhealingworldpeacepoetry.com

Inner Child Press Anthologies

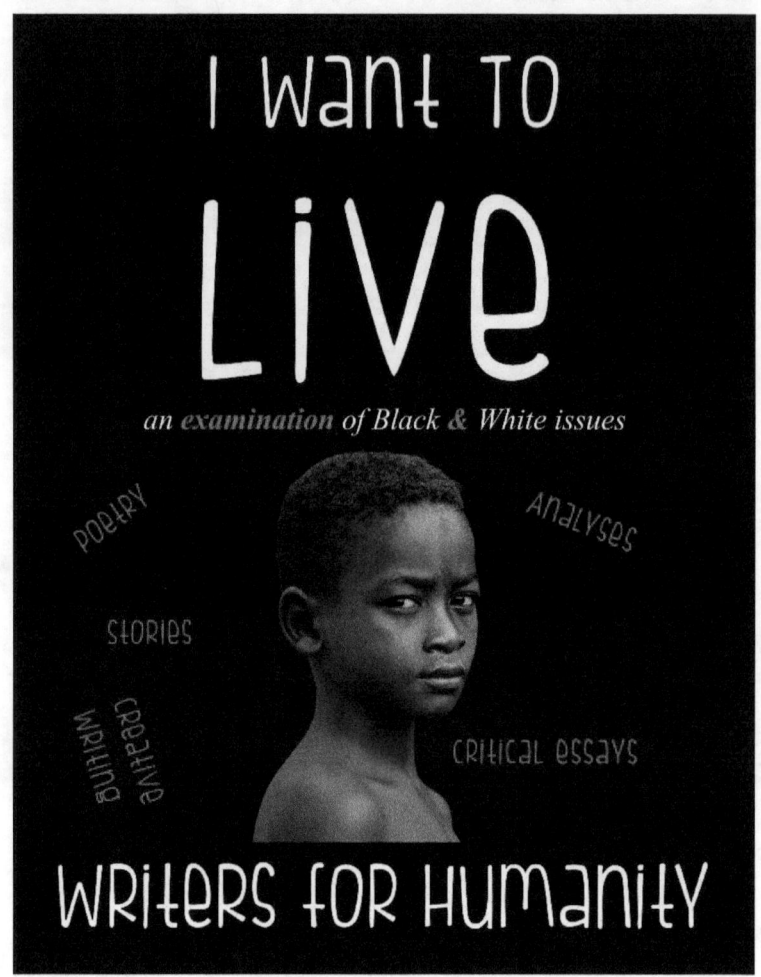

Now Available
www.innerchildpress.com

Inner Child Press Anthologies

Inner Child Press International
&
The Year of the Poet
present

Poetry
the best of 2020

Poets of the World

Now Available
www.innerchildpress.com

Inner Child Press Anthologies

Inner Child Press International

presents

W.A.R.

We Are Revolution

Poets for Humanity

Now Available
www.innerchildpress.com

Inner Child Press Anthologies

Now Available
www.innerchildpress.com

Inner Child Press Anthologies

Now Available
www.innerchildpress.com

Inner Child Press Anthologies

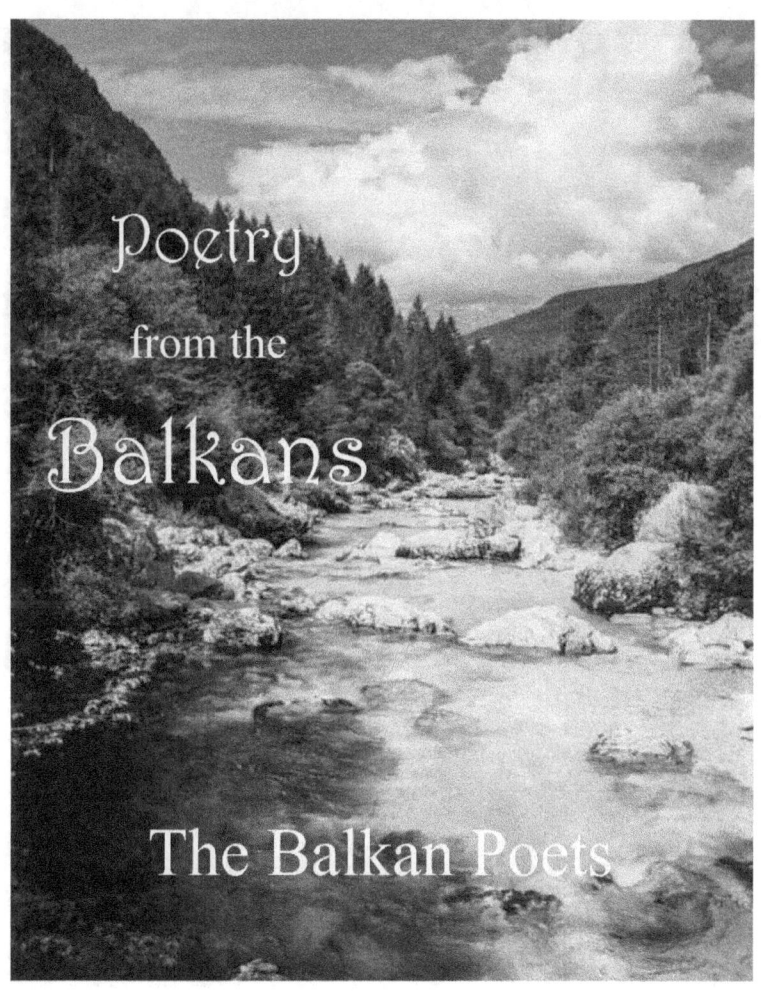

Now Available at
www.innerchildpress.com

Inner Child Press Anthologies

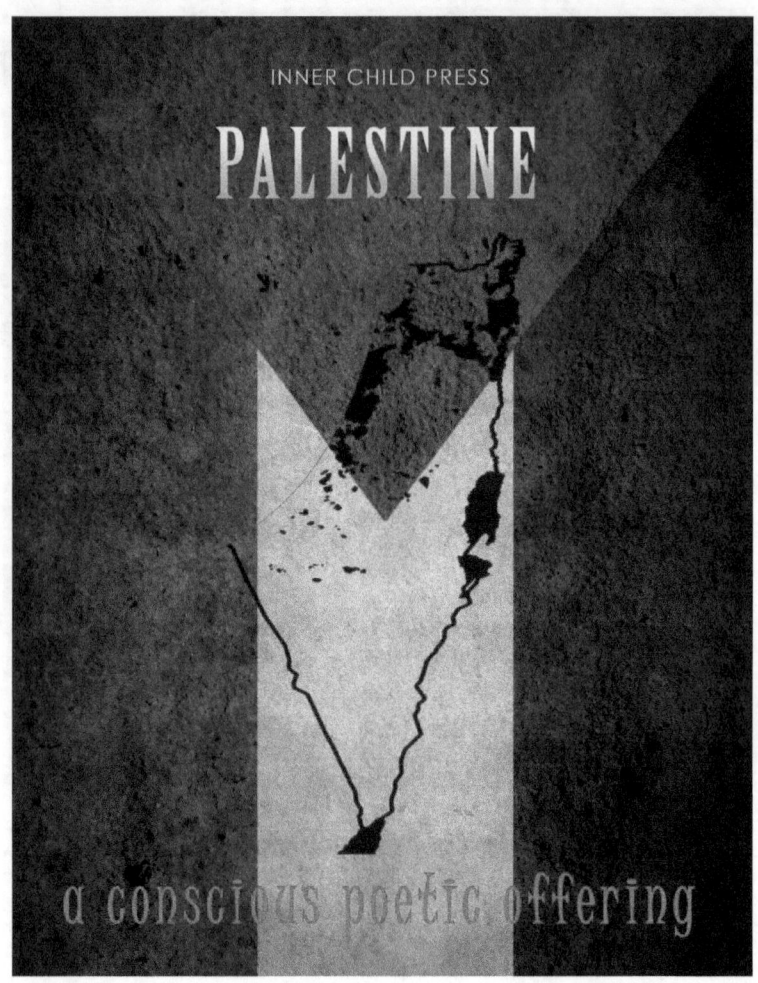

Now Available at
www.innerchildpress.com

Inner Child Press Anthologies

Now Available at
www.innerchildpress.com

Inner Child Press Anthologies

Now Available
www.worldhealingworldpeacepoetry.com

Inner Child Press Anthologies

Now Available
www.worldhealingworldpeacepoetry.com

Inner Child Press Anthologies

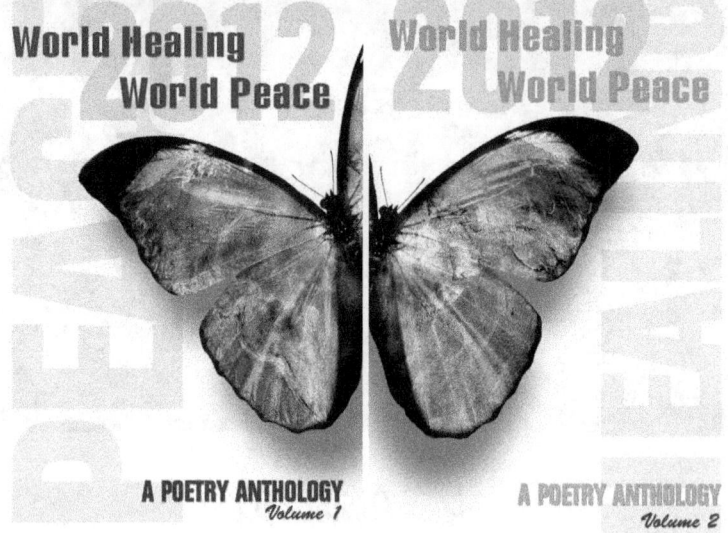

Now Available
www.worldhealingworldpeacepoetry.com

Inner Child Press Anthologies

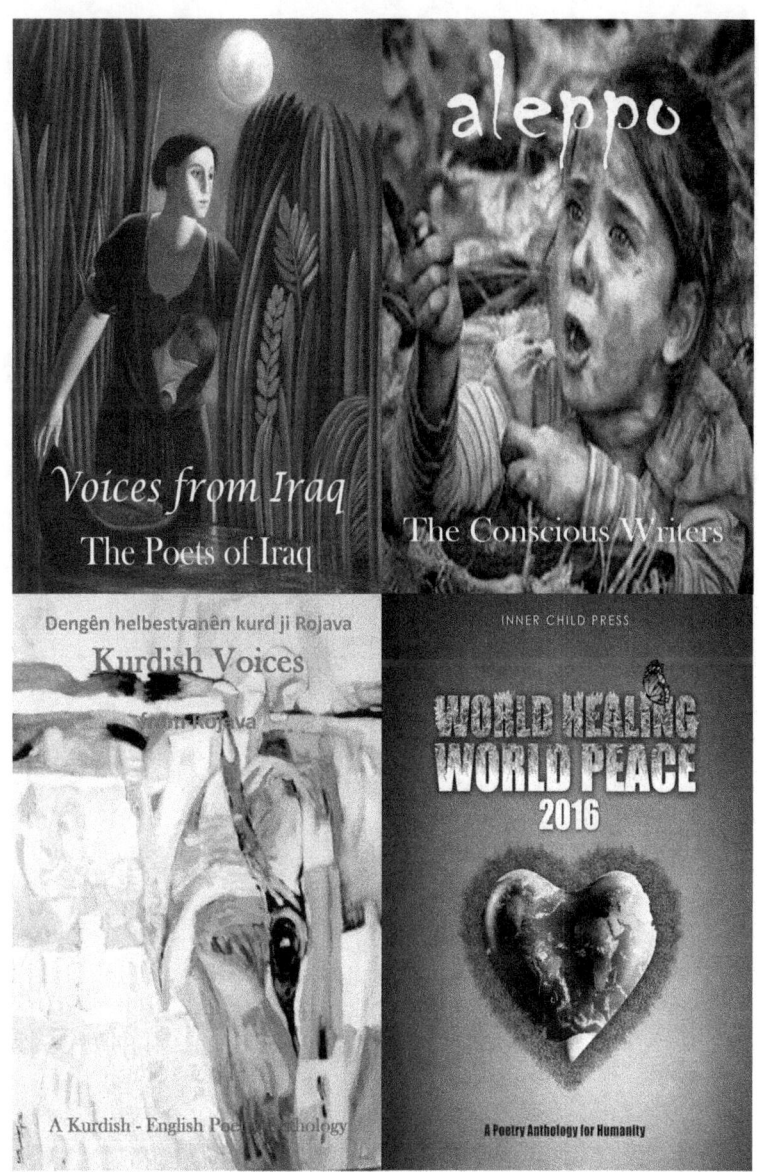

Now Available
www.innerchildpress.com/anthologies

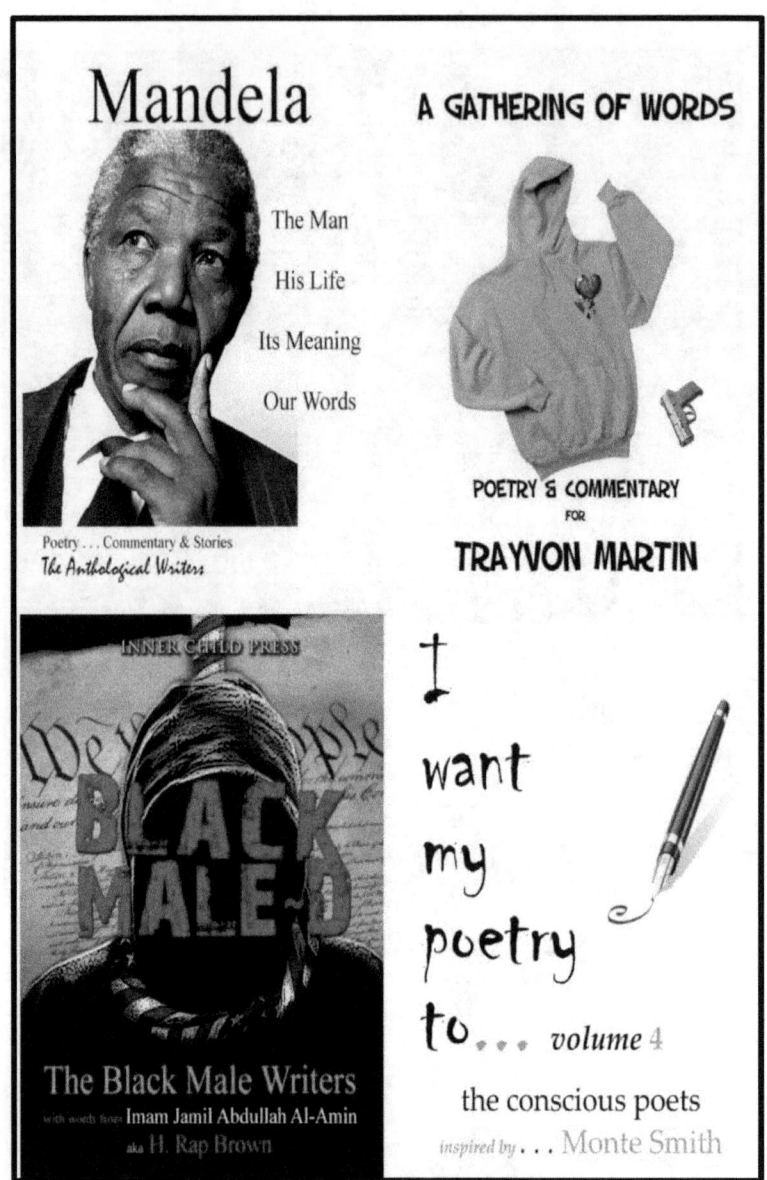

Inner Child Press Anthologies

Now Available
www.innerchildpress.com/anthologies

Inner Child Press Anthologies

Now Available
www.innerchildpress.com/anthologies

Inner Child Press Anthologies

Now Available
www.innerchildpress.com/anthologies

Inner Child Press Anthologies

Now Available

www.innerchildpress.com/the-year-of-the-poet

Inner Child Press Anthologies

Now Available

www.innerchildpress.com/the-year-of-the-poet

Inner Child Press Anthologies

Now Available
www.innerchildpress.com/the-year-of-the-poet

Inner Child Press Anthologies

Now Available

www.innerchildpress.com/the-year-of-the-poet

Inner Child Press Anthologies

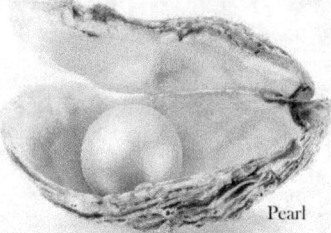
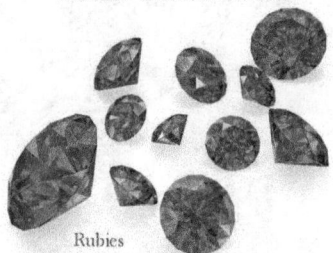

Now Available

www.innerchildpress.com/the-year-of-the-poet

Inner Child Press Anthologies

Now Available

www.innerchildpress.com/the-year-of-the-poet

Inner Child Press Anthologies

Now Available
www.innerchildpress.com/the-year-of-the-poet

Inner Child Press Anthologies

Now Available
www.innerchildpress.com/the-year-of-the-poet

Inner Child Press Anthologies

Now Available
www.innerchildpress.com/the-year-of-the-poet

Inner Child Press Anthologies

Now Available
www.innerchildpress.com/the-year-of-the-poet

Inner Child Press Anthologies

Now Available
www.innerchildpress.com/the-year-of-the-poet

Inner Child Press Anthologies

The Year of the Poet IV
September 2017

Featured Poets
Martina Reisz Newberry
Ameer Nassir
Christine Fulco Neal
Robert Neal

The Elm Tree

The Poetry Posse 2017

Gail Weston Shazor * Caroline Nazareno * Bismay Mohanty
Teresa E. Gallion * Anna Jakubczak Vel Ratty Adalan
Joe DaVerbal Minddancer * Shareef Abdur – Rasheed
Albert Carrasco * Kimberly Burnham * Elizabeth Castillo
Hülya N. Yılmaz * Faleeha Hassan * Jackie Davis Allen
Jen Walls * Nizar Sartawi * * William S. Peters, Sr.

The Year of the Poet IV
October 2017

Featured Poets
Ahmed Abu Saleem
Nedal Al-Qaeim
Sadeddin Shahin

The Black Walnut Tree

The Poetry Posse 2017

Gail Weston Shazor * Caroline Nazareno * Bismay Mohanty
Teresa E. Gallion * Anna Jakubczak Vel Ratty Adalan
Joe DaVerbal Minddancer * Shareef Abdur – Rasheed
Albert Carrasco * Kimberly Burnham * Elizabeth Castillo
Hülya N. Yılmaz * Faleeha Hassan * Jackie Davis Allen
Jen Walls * Nizar Sartawi * * William S. Peters, Sr.

The Year of the Poet IV
November 2017

Featured Poets
Kay Peters
Alfreda D. Ghee
Gabriella Garofalo
Rosemary Cappello

The Tree of Life

The Poetry Posse 2017

Gail Weston Shazor * Caroline Nazareno * Bismay Mohanty
Teresa E. Gallion * Anna Jakubczak Vel Ratty Adalan
Joe DaVerbal Minddancer * Shareef Abdur – Rasheed
Albert Carrasco * Kimberly Burnham * Elizabeth Castillo
Hülya N. Yılmaz * Faleeha Hassan * Jackie Davis Allen
Jen Walls * Nizar Sartawi * William S. Peters, Sr.

The Year of the Poet IV
December 2017

Featured Poets
Justice Clarke
Mariel M. Pabroa
Kiley Brown

The Fig Tree

The Poetry Posse 2017

Gail Weston Shazor * Caroline Nazareno * Bismay Mohanty
Teresa E. Gallion * Anna Jakubczak Vel Ratty Adalan
Joe DaVerbal Minddancer * Shareef Abdur – Rasheed
Albert Carrasco * Kimberly Burnham * Elizabeth Castillo
Hülya N. Yılmaz * Faleeha Hassan * Jackie Davis Allen
Jen Walls * Nizar Sartawi * William S. Peters, Sr.

Now Available
www.innerchildpress.com/the-year-of-the-poet

Inner Child Press Anthologies

Now Available
www.innerchildpress.com/the-year-of-the-poet

Inner Child Press Anthologies

Now Available

www.innerchildpress.com/the-year-of-the-poet

Inner Child Press Anthologies

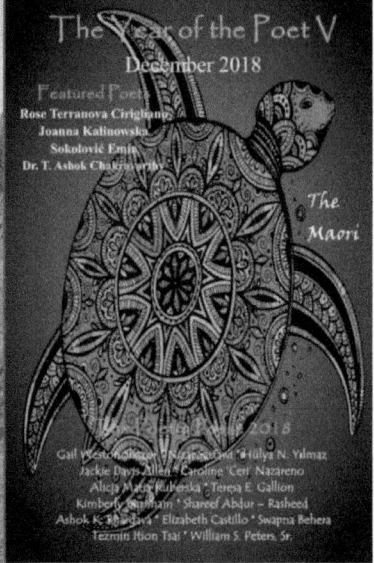

Now Available
www.innerchildpress.com/the-year-of-the-poet

Inner Child Press Anthologies

The Year of the Poet VI
January 2019

Indigenous North Americans

Featured Poets
Honda Elfchtali
Anthony Briscoe
Iram Fatima 'Ashi'
Dr. K. K. Mathew

Dream Catcher

The Poetry Posse 2019

Gail Weston Shazor * Joe Paire * Hülya N. Yılmaz
Jackie Davis Allen * Caroline 'Ceri' Nazareno
Alicja Maria Kuberska * Teresa E. Gallion
Kimberly Burnham * Shareef Abdur – Rasheed
Ashok K. Bhargava * Elizabeth Castillo * Swapna Behera
Tezmin Ition Tsai * William S. Peters, Sr.

The Year of the Poet VI
February 2019

Featured Poets
Marek Lukaszewicz * Bharati Nayak
Aida G. Roque * Jean-Jacques Fournier

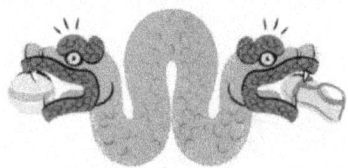

Meso-America

The Poetry Posse 2019

Gail Weston Shazor * Albert Carrasco * Hülya N. Yılmaz
Jackie Davis Allen * Caroline Nazareno * Eliza Segiet
Alicja Maria Kuberska * Teresa E. Gallion * Joe Paire
Kimberly Burnham * Shareef Abdur – Rasheed
Ashok K. Bhargava * Elizabeth Castillo * Swapna Behera
Tezmin Ition Tsai * William S. Peters, Sr.

The Year of the Poet VI
March 2019

Featured Poets
Enesa Mahmić * Sylwia K. Malinowska
Shurouk Hammoud * Anwer Ghani

The Caribbean

The Poetry Posse 2019

Gail Weston Shazor * Albert Carrasco * Hülya N. Yılmaz
Jackie Davis Allen * Caroline Nazareno * Eliza Segiet
Alicja Maria Kuberska * Teresa E. Gallion * Joe Paire
Kimberly Burnham * Shareef Abdur – Rasheed
Ashok K. Bhargava * Elizabeth Castillo * Swapna Behera
Tezmin Ition Tsai * William S. Peters, Sr.

The Year of the Poet VI
April 2019

Featured Poets
DL Davis * Michelle Joan Barulich
Luljeta Haziri * Faleeha Hassan

Central & West Africa

The Poetry Posse 2019

Gail Weston Shazor * Albert Carrasco * Hülya N. Yılmaz
Jackie Davis Allen * Caroline Nazareno * Eliza Segiet
Alicja Maria Kuberska * Teresa E. Gallion * Joe Paire
Kimberly Burnham * Shareef Abdur – Rasheed
Ashok K. Bhargava * Elizabeth Castillo * Swapna Behera
Tezmin Ition Tsai * William S. Peters, Sr.

Now Available

www.innerchildpress.com/the-year-of-the-poet

Inner Child Press Anthologies

Now Available

www.innerchildpress.com/the-year-of-the-poet

Inner Child Press Anthologies

Now Available
www.innerchildpress.com/the-year-of-the-poet

Inner Child Press Anthologies

Now Available
www.innerchildpress.com/the-year-of-the-poet

Inner Child Press Anthologies

The Year of the Poet VII
September 2020

Featured Poets
Raed Anis Al-Jishi • Sofiyonviz Nuchana
Dr. Brajesh Kumar Gupta • Umid Najjari

Mikhail Sergeyevich Gorbachev ~ 1990

The Year of Peace
Celebrating past Nobel Peace Prize Recipients

The Poetry Posse 2020
Gail Weston Shazor • Albert Carasco • Hülya N. Yılmaz
Jackie Davis Allen • Caroline Nazareno • Eliza Segiet
Alicja Maria Kuberska • Teresa E. Gallion • Joe Paire
Kimberly Burnham • Shareef Abdur-Rasheed
Ashok K. Bhargava • Elizabeth Castillo • Swapna Behera
Tezmin Ition Tsai • William S. Peters, Sr.

The Year of the Poet VII
October 2020

Featured Poets
Mutawaf A. Shaheed • Galina Italyanskaya
Nadeem Fraz • Avril Tanya Meallem

Kim Dae-jung ~ 2000

The Year of Peace
Celebrating past Nobel Peace Prize Recipients

The Poetry Posse 2020
Gail Weston Shazor • Albert Carasco • Hülya N. Yılmaz
Jackie Davis Allen • Caroline Nazareno • Eliza Segiet
Alicja Maria Kuberska • Teresa E. Gallion • Joe Paire
Kimberly Burnham • Shareef Abdur-Rasheed
Ashok K. Bhargava • Elizabeth Castillo • Swapna Behera
Tezmin Ition Tsai • William S. Peters, Sr.

The Year of the Poet VII
November 2020

Featured Poets
Elisa Mascia • Sue Lindenberg McClelland
Hatif Janabi • Ivan Gacina

Liu Xiaobo ~ 2010

The Year of Peace
Celebrating past Nobel Peace Prize Recipients

The Poetry Posse 2020
Gail Weston Shazor • Albert Carasco • Hülya N. Yılmaz
Jackie Davis Allen • Caroline Nazareno • Eliza Segiet
Alicja Maria Kuberska • Teresa E. Gallion • Joe Paire
Kimberly Burnham • Shareef Abdur-Rasheed
Ashok K. Bhargava • Elizabeth Castillo • Swapna Behera
Tezmin Ition Tsai • William S. Peters, Sr.

The Year of the Poet VII
December 2020

Featured Poets
Ratan Ghosh • Ibtisam Ibrahim Al-Asady
Brindha Vinodh • Selma Kopic

Abiy Ahmed Ali ~ 2019

The Year of Peace
Celebrating past Nobel Peace Prize Recipients

The Poetry Posse 2020
Gail Weston Shazor • Albert Carasco • Hülya N. Yılmaz
Jackie Davis Allen • Caroline Nazareno • Eliza Segiet
Alicja Maria Kuberska • Teresa E. Gallion • Joe Paire
Kimberly Burnham • Shareef Abdur-Rasheed
Ashok K. Bhargava • Elizabeth Castillo • Swapna Behera
Tezmin Ition Tsai • William S. Peters, Sr.

Now Available
www.innerchildpress.com/the-year-of-the-poet

Inner Child Press Anthologies

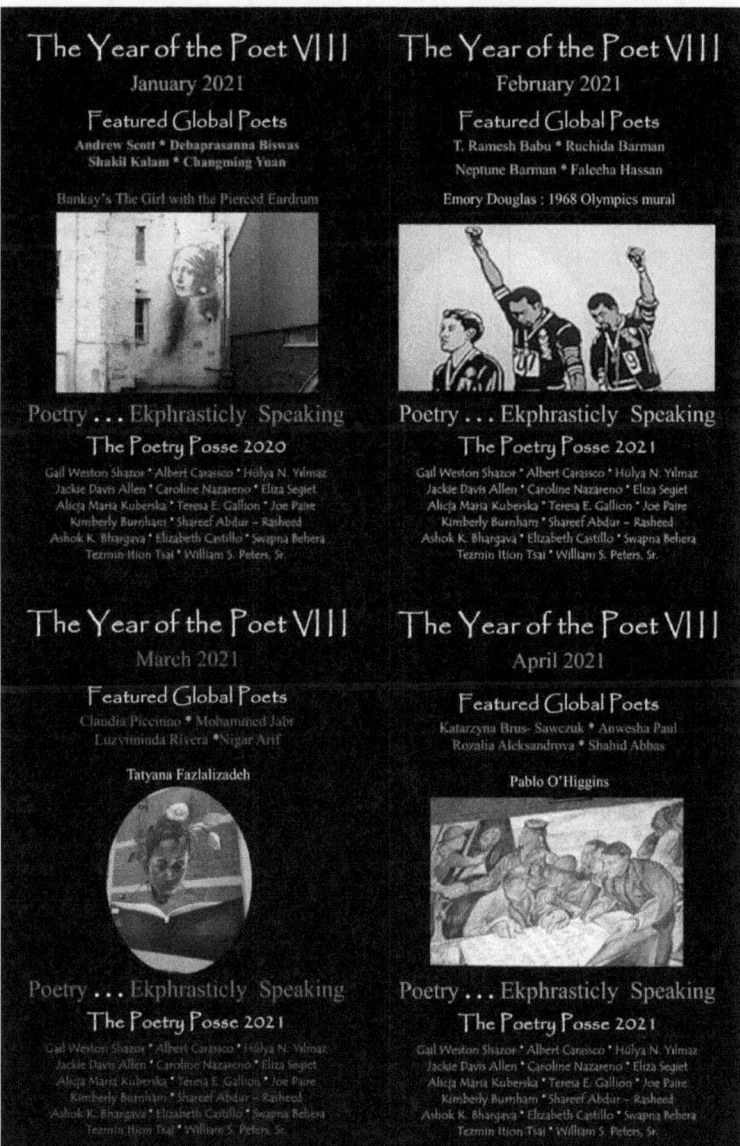

Now Available

www.innerchildpress.com/the-year-of-the-poet

Inner Child Press Anthologies

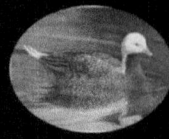
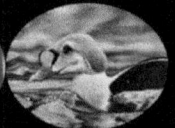
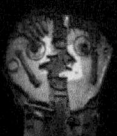

Now Available

www.innerchildpress.com/the-year-of-the-poet

Inner Child Press Anthologies

The Year of the Poet VIII
September 2021

Featured Global Poets
Monsif Beroual * Sandesh Ghimire
Sharmila Poudel * Pavol Janik

Heather Jansch

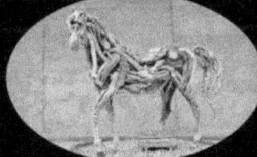

Poetry ... Ekphrasticly Speaking

The Poetry Posse 2021

Gail Weston Shazor * Albert Carasco * Hülya N. Yılmaz
Jackie Davis Allen * Caroline Nazareno * Eliza Segiet
Alicja Maria Kuberska * Teresa E. Gallion * Joe Paire
Kimberly Burnham * Shareef Abdur – Rasheed
Ashok K. Bhargava * Elizabeth Castillo * Swapna Behera
Tezmin Ition Tsai * William S. Peters, Sr.

The Year of the Poet VIII
October 2021

Featured Global Poets
C. E. Shy * Saswata Ganguly
Suranjit Gain * Hasiba Hilal

Dale Lamphere

Poetry ... Ekphrasticly Speaking

The Poetry Posse 2021

Gail Weston Shazor * Albert Carasco * Hülya N. Yılmaz
Jackie Davis Allen * Caroline Nazareno * Eliza Segiet
Alicja Maria Kuberska * Teresa E. Gallion * Joe Paire
Kimberly Burnham * Shareef Abdur – Rasheed
Ashok K. Bhargava * Elizabeth Castillo * Swapna Behera
Tezmin Ition Tsai * William S. Peters, Sr.

The Year of the Poet VIII
November 2021

Featured Global Poets
Errol D. Bean * Ibrahim Honjo
Tanja Ajtic * Rajashree Mohapatra

Andy Goldsworthy

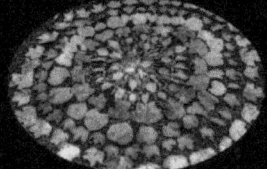

Poetry ... Ekphrasticly Speaking

The Poetry Posse 2021

Gail Weston Shazor * Albert Carasco * Hülya N. Yılmaz
Jackie Davis Allen * Caroline Nazareno * Eliza Segiet
Alicja Maria Kuberska * Teresa E. Gallion * Joe Paire
Kimberly Burnham * Shareef Abdur – Rasheed
Ashok K. Bhargava * Elizabeth Castillo * Swapna Behera
Tezmin Ition Tsai * William S. Peters, Sr.

The Year of the Poet VIII
December 2021

Featured Global Poets
Orbinda Ganga * Fadairo Tesleem
Anthony Arnold * Iyad Shamasnah

Fredric Edwin Church

Poetry ... Ekphrasticly Speaking

The Poetry Posse 2021

Gail Weston Shazor * Albert Carasco * Hülya N. Yılmaz
Jackie Davis Allen * Caroline Nazareno * Eliza Segiet
Alicja Maria Kuberska * Teresa E. Gallion * Joe Paire
Kimberly Burnham * Shareef Abdur – Rasheed
Ashok K. Bhargava * Elizabeth Castillo * Swapna Behera
Tezmin Ition Tsai * William S. Peters, Sr.

Now Available
www.innerchildpress.com/the-year-of-the-poet

Inner Child Press Anthologies

The Year of the Poet IX
January 2022

Featured Global Poets
Ratan Ghosh * Christine Neil-Wright
Andrew Scott * Ashok Kumar

Climate Change : The Ice Cap

Poetry . . . Ekphrasticly Speaking

The Poetry Posse 2021

Gail Weston Shazor * Albert Carasco * Hülya N. Yılmaz
Jackie Davis Allen * Caroline Nazareno * Eliza Segiet
Alicja Maria Kuberska * Teresa E. Gallion * Joe Paire
Kimberly Burnham * Shareef Abdur – Rasheed
Ashok K. Bhargava * Elizabeth Castillo * Swapna Behera
Tezmin Ition Tsai * William S. Peters, Sr.

The Year of the Poet IX
February 2022

Featured Global Poets
Roza Boyanova * Ramón de Jesús Núñez Duval
Mammad Ismayil * Tarana Turan Rahimli

Climate Change and Mountains

Poetry . . . Ekphrasticly Speaking

The Poetry Posse 2021

Gail Weston Shazor * Albert Carasco * Hülya N. Yılmaz
Jackie Davis Allen * Caroline Nazareno * Eliza Segiet
Alicja Maria Kuberska * Teresa E. Gallion * Joe Paire
Kimberly Burnham * Shareef Abdur – Rasheed
Ashok K. Bhargava * Elizabeth Castillo * Swapna Behera
Tezmin Ition Tsai * William S. Peters, Sr.

The Year of the Poet IX
March 2022

Featured Global Poets
Dimitris P. Kraniotis * Marlene Pasini
Kennedy Ochieng * Swayam Prashant

Climate Change and Space Debris

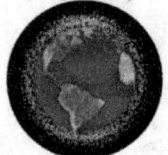

Poetry . . . Ekphrasticly Speaking

The Poetry Posse 2021

Gail Weston Shazor * Albert Carasco * Hülya N. Yılmaz
Jackie Davis Allen * Caroline Nazareno * Eliza Segiet
Alicja Maria Kuberska * Teresa E. Gallion * Joe Paire
Kimberly Burnham * Shareef Abdur – Rasheed
Ashok K. Bhargava * Elizabeth Castillo * Swapna Behera
Tezmin Ition Tsai * William S. Peters, Sr.

The Year of the Poet IX
April 2022

Featured Global Poets
Alonzo Gross * Dr. Debaprasanna Biswas
Monsif Beroual * Carol Aronoff

Climate Change and Oceans

*Celebrating our 100th Edition *

Poetry . . . Ekphrasticly Speaking

The Poetry Posse 2021

Gail Weston Shazor * Albert Carasco * Hülya N. Yılmaz
Jackie Davis Allen * Caroline Nazareno * Eliza Segiet
Alicja Maria Kuberska * Teresa E. Gallion * Joe Paire
Kimberly Burnham * Shareef Abdur – Rasheed
Ashok K. Bhargava * Elizabeth Castillo * Swapna Behera
Tezmin Ition Tsai * William S. Peters, Sr.

Now Available

www.innerchildpress.com/the-year-of-the-poet

Inner Child Press Anthologies

The Year of the Poet IX
May 2022

Featured Global Poets
Ndaba Sibanda * Smrutiranjan Mohanty
Ajanta Paul * Monalisa Dash Dwibedy

Climate Change and Birds

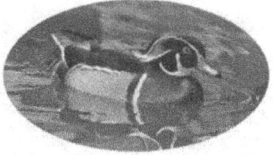

Poetry . . . Ekphrasticly Speaking

The Poetry Posse 2021

Gail Weston Shazor * Albert Carasco * Hülya N. Yılmaz
Jackie Davis Allen * Caroline Nazareno * Eliza Segiet
Alicja Maria Kuberska * Teresa E. Gallion * Joe Paire
Kimberly Burnham * Shareef Abdur – Rasheed
Ashok K. Bhargava * Elizabeth Castillo * Swapna Behera
Tezmin Ition Tsai * William S. Peters, Sr.

The Year of the Poet IX
June 2022

Featured Global Poets
Yuan Changming * Azeezat Okunlola
Tanja Ajtić * Philip Chijioke Abonyi

Climate Change and Trees

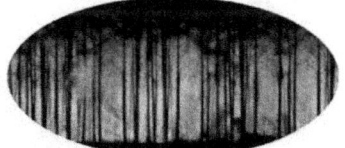

Poetry . . . Ekphrasticly Speaking

The Poetry Posse 2022

Gail Weston Shazor * Albert Carasco * Hülya N. Yılmaz
Jackie Davis Allen * Caroline Nazareno * Eliza Segiet
Alicja Maria Kuberska * Teresa E. Gallion * Joe Paire
Kimberly Burnham * Shareef Abdur – Rasheed
Ashok K. Bhargava * Elizabeth Castillo * Swapna Behera
Tezmin Ition Tsai * William S. Peters, Sr.

The Year of the Poet IX
July 2022

Featured Global Poets
Michelle Joan Barulich * Mili Das
Anna Ferriero * Ujjal Mandal

Climate Change and Animals

Poetry . . . Ekphrasticly Speaking

The Poetry Posse 2022

Gail Weston Shazor * Albert Carasco * Hülya N. Yılmaz
Jackie Davis Allen * Caroline Nazareno * Eliza Segiet
Alicja Maria Kuberska * Teresa E. Gallion * Joe Paire
Kimberly Burnham * Shareef Abdur – Rasheed
Ashok K. Bhargava * Elizabeth Castillo * Swapna Behera
Tezmin Ition Tsai * William S. Peters, Sr.

The Year of the Poet IX
August 2022

Featured Global Poets
Pankhuri Sinha * Abdulloh Abdumominov
Caroline Turunç * Tali Cohen Shahtai

Climate Change and Agriculture

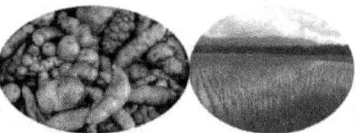

Poetry . . . Ekphrasticly Speaking

The Poetry Posse 2022

Gail Weston Shazor * Albert Carasco * Hülya N. Yılmaz
Jackie Davis Allen * Caroline Nazareno * Eliza Segiet
Alicja Maria Kuberska * Teresa E. Gallion * Joe Paire
Kimberly Burnham * Shareef Abdur – Rasheed
Ashok K. Bhargava * Elizabeth Castillo * Swapna Behera
Tezmin Ition Tsai * William S. Peters, Sr.

Now Available

www.innerchildpress.com/the-year-of-the-poet

Inner Child Press Anthologies

The Year of the Poet IX
September 2022

Featured Global Poets

Ngozi Olivia Osuoha * Biswajit Mishra
Sylwia K. Malinowska * Sajid Hussein

Climate Change and Wind and Weather Patterns

Poetry ... Ekphrasticly Speaking

The Poetry Posse 2022

Gail Weston Shazor * Albert Carasco * Hülya N. Yılmaz
Jackie Davis Allen * Caroline Nazareno * Eliza Segiet
Alicja Maria KubersKa * Teresa E. Gallion * Joe Paire
Kimberly Burnham * Shareef Abdur – Rasheed
Ashok K. Bhargava * Elizabeth Castillo * Swapna Behera
Tezmin Ition Tsai * William S. Peters, Sr.

The Year of the Poet IX
October 2022

Featured Global Poets

Andrew Kouroupos * Brenda Mohammed
Carthornia Kouroupos * Faleeha Hassan

Climate Change and Oil and Power

Poetry ... Ekphrasticly Speaking

The Poetry Posse 2022

Gail Weston Shazor * Albert Carasco * Hülya N. Yılmaz
Jackie Davis Allen * Caroline Nazareno * Eliza Segiet
Alicja Maria Kubersa * Teresa E. Gallion * Joe Paire
Kimberly Burnham * Shareef Abdur – Rasheed
Ashok K. Bhargava * Elizabeth Castillo * Swapna Behera
Tezmin Ition Tsai * William S. Peters, Sr.

The Year of the Poet IX
November 2022

Featured Global Poets

Hema Ravi * Shafkat Aziz Hajam
Selma Kopic * Ibrahim Honjo

Climate Change : Time to Act

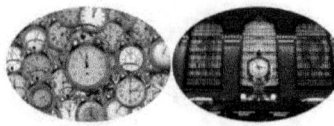

Poetry ... Ekphrasticly Speaking

The Poetry Posse 2022

Gail Weston Shazor * Albert Carasco * Hülya N. Yılmaz
Jackie Davis Allen * Caroline Nazareno * Eliza Segiet
Alicja Maria Kuberska * Teresa E. Gallion * Joe Paire
Kimberly Burnham * Shareef Abdur – Rasheed
Ashok K. Bhargava * Elizabeth Castillo * Swapna Behera
Tezmin Ition Tsai * William S. Peters, Sr.

The Year of the Poet IX
December 2022

Featured Global Poets

Elarbi Abdelfattah * Lorraine Cragg
Neha Bhandarkar * Robert Gibbons

Climate Change Bees, Butterflies and Insect Life

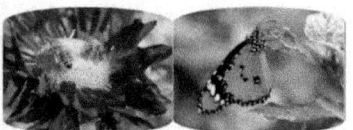

Poetry ... Ekphrasticly Speaking

The Poetry Posse 2022

Gail Weston Shazor * Albert Carasco * Hülya N. Yılmaz
Jackie Davis Allen * Caroline Nazareno * Eliza Segiet
Alicja Maria Kuberska * Teresa E. Gallion * Joe Paire
Kimberly Burnham * Shareef Abdur – Rasheed
Ashok K. Bhargava * Elizabeth Castillo * Swapna Behera
Tezmin Ition Tsai * William S. Peters, Sr.

Now Available

www.innerchildpress.com/the-year-of-the-poet

Inner Child Press Anthologies

Now Available

www.innerchildpress.com/the-year-of-the-poet

Inner Child Press Anthologies

The Year of the Poet X
September 2023

Featured Global Poets
Eftichia Karpadeli * Chinh Nguyen
Nigar Agalarova * Carmela Cueva

Children : Difference Makers

~ Easton LaChappelle ~

The Poetry Posse 2023
Gail Weston Shazor * Albert Carasco * Hülya N. Yılmaz
Jackie Davis Allen * Caroline Nazareno * Kimberly Burnham
Alicja Maria Kuberska * Teresa E. Gallion * Joe Paire
Michelle Joan Barulich * Shareef Abdur – Rasheed
Ashok K. Bhargava * Elizabeth Castillo * Swapna Behera
Tezmin Ition Tsai * Eliza Segiet * William S. Peters, Sr.

The Year of the Poet X
October 2023

Featured Global Poets
CSP Shrivastava * Huniie Parker
Noreen Snyder * Ramkrishna Paul

Children : Difference Makers

~ Malala Yousafzai ~

The Poetry Posse 2023
Gail Weston Shazor * Albert Carasco * Hülya N. Yılmaz
Jackie Davis Allen * Caroline Nazareno * Kimberly Burnham
Alicja Maria Kuberska * Teresa E. Gallion * Joe Paire
Michelle Joan Barulich * Shareef Abdur – Rasheed
Ashok K. Bhargava * Elizabeth Castillo * Swapna Behera
Tezmin Ition Tsai * Eliza Segiet * William S. Peters, Sr.

The Year of the Poet X
November 2023

Featured Global Poets
Ibrahim Honjo * Balachandran Nair
Xanthi Hondrou-Hil * Francesco Favetta

Children : Difference Makers

~ Jean-Michel Basquiat ~

The Poetry Posse 2023
Gail Weston Shazor * Albert Carasco * Hülya N. Yılmaz
Jackie Davis Allen * Caroline Nazareno * Kimberly Burnham
Alicja Maria Kuberska * Teresa E. Gallion * Joe Paire
Michelle Joan Barulich * Shareef Abdur – Rasheed
Ashok K. Bhargava * Elizabeth Castillo * Swapna Behera
Tezmin Ition Tsai * Eliza Segiet * William S. Peters, Sr.

The Year of the Poet X
December 2023

Featured Global Poets
Caroline Laurent Turunc * Neha Bhandarkar
Shafkat Aziz Hajam * Elarbi Abdelfattah

Children : Difference Makers

~ Melati and Isabel Wijsen ~

The Poetry Posse 2023
Gail Weston Shazor * Albert Carasco * Hülya N. Yılmaz
Jackie Davis Allen * Caroline Nazareno * Kimberly Burnham
Alicja Maria Kuberska * Teresa E. Gallion * Joe Paire
Michelle Joan Barulich * Shareef Abdur – Rasheed
Ashok K. Bhargava * Elizabeth Castillo * Swapna Behera
Tezmin Ition Tsai * Eliza Segiet * William S. Peters, Sr.

Now Available
www.innerchildpress.com/the-year-of-the-poet

and there is much, much more !

visit . . .

www.innerchildpress.com/anthologies-sales-special.php

Also check out our Authors and all the wonderful Books Available at :

www.innerchildpress.com/authors-pages

Now Available

www.worldhealingworldpeacepoetry.com

Now Available

www.worldhealingworldpeacepoetry.com

www.worldhealingworldpeacepoetry.com

World Healing World Peace
2012, 2014, 2016, 2018, 2020, 2022

Now Available

www.worldhealingworldpeacepoetry.com

Inner Child Press International

'building bridges of cultural understanding'

Meet the Board of Directors

William S. Peters, Sr.
Chair Person
Founder
Inner Child Enterprises
Inner Child Press

Hülya N Yılmaz
Director
Editing Services
Co-Chair Person

Fahredin B. Shehu
Director
Cultural Affairs

Elizabeth E. Castillo
Director
Recording Secretary

De'Andre Hawthorne
Director
Performance Poetry

Gail Weston Shazor
Director
Anthologies

Kimberly Burnham
Director
Cultural Ambassador
Pacific Northwest
USA

Ashok K. Bhargava
Director
WIN Awards

Deborah Smart
Director
Publicity
Marketing

www.innerchildpress.com

Inner Child Press International
'building bridges of cultural understanding'

Meet our Cultural Ambassadors

Fahredin Shehu
Director of Cultural

Fatcha Hassan
Iraq - USA

Elizabeth E. Castillo
Philippines

Antoinette Coleman
Chicago
Midwest USA

Ananda Nepali
Nepal - Tibet
Northern India

Kimberly Burnham
Pacific Northwest
USA

Alicja Kuberska
Poland
Eastern Europe

Swapna Behera
India
Southeast Asia

Kolade O. Freedom
Nigeria
West Africa

Monsif Beroual
Morocco
Northern Africa

Ashok K. Bhargava
Canada

Tzemin Ition Tsai
Republic of China
Greater China

Alicia M. Ramírez
Mexico
Central America

Christena AV Williams
Jamaica
Caribbean

Louise Hudon
Eastern Canada

Aziz Mountassir
Morocco
Northern Africa

Shareef Abdur-Rasheed
Southeastern USA

Laure Charazac
France
Western Europe

Mohammad Ikbal Harb
Lebanon
Middle East

Mohamed Abdel Aziz Shmeis
Egypt
Middle East

Hilary Mainga
Kenya
Eastern Africa

Josephus R. Johnson
Liberia

www.innerchildpress.com

This Anthological Publication
is underwritten solely by

Inner Child Press International

Inner Child Press is a Publishing Company Founded and Operated by Writers. Our personal publishing experiences provides us an intimate understanding of the sometimes daunting challenges Writers, New and Seasoned may face in the Business of Publishing and Marketing their Creative "Written Work".

For more Information

Inner Child Press International

www.innerchildpress.com

'building bridges of cultural understanding'
202 Wiltree Court, State College, Pennsylvania 16801

www.innerchildpress.com

~ fini ~

www.ingramcontent.com/pod-product-compliance
Lightning Source LLC
LaVergne TN
LVHW051043080426
835508LV00019B/1673